PENGUIN BOOKS

HONOR TO THE BRIDE

Jane Kramer has been a writer for *The New Yorker* since 1964. She is the author of *Off Washington Square*, *Allen Ginsberg in America*, *The Last Cowboy*, *Unsettling Europe*, and *Europeans*. In 1981, she won the American Book Award for Non-fiction. She is married to the anthropologist Vincent Crapanzano, and they have a daughter, Aleksandra. She lives with her family in Paris and New York.

HONOR TO THE BRIDE

Like the Pigeon that Guards its Grain Under the Clove Tree

JANE KRAMER

PENGUIN BOOKS

PENGUIN BOOKS
Published by the Penguin Group
Viking Penguin, a division of Penguin Books USA Inc.,
40 West 23rd Street, New York, New York 10010, U.S.A.
Penguin Books Ltd, 27 Wrights Lane, London W8 5TZ, England
Penguin Books Australia Ltd, Ringwood, Victoria, Australia
Penguin Books Canada Ltd, 2801 John Street,
Markham, Ontario, Canada L3R 1B4
Penguin Books (N.Z.) Ltd, 182–190 Wairau Road,
Auckland 10, New Zealand

Penguin Books Ltd, Registered Offices:
Harmondsworth, Middlesex, England

First published in the United States of America by
Farrar, Straus & Giroux, Inc. 1970
Published in Penguin Books 1990

1   3   5   7   9   10   8   6   4   2

The text of this book
originally appeared in *The New Yorker*.

ISBN 0 14 01.2896 4
(CIP data available)

Printed in the United States of America

To
SEVERIN D'AIGUILLETTE

CONTENTS

Honor
to the Bride

In Morocco, this story would probably be called a love story. It took place one year when I was living in that country, and it concerned an Arab by the name of Omar ben Allel, his wife, Dawia, and their thirteen-year-old daughter, Khadija, who was lost on a pilgrimage in June, found in a brothel in July, and properly married off in August. They were by no means exceptional Moroccans. Nor was their story really an exceptional one. It was sentimental, complicated, cruel, and a little crazy, but it was a thoroughly Arab story,

3

and it plodded along in time like an awkward arabesque, always elaborating on itself and never appearing to be going anywhere. Its lessons were the familiar lessons of shame, face, favors, and the pocketbook. And its moral was simply that everything in the end depends on Allah's great and inexplicable will. Most Moroccans would say that it was too mundane to bear retelling. By the time I left the country, Omar himself was starting to forget the details.

Omar and Dawia came from a tiny tribal village in northern Morocco, but, like hundreds of thousands of other Arab *fellaha* whose tribal land was broken up during the French protectorate, they had drifted out of the countryside and into one of the sprawling urban squatter settlements that the French call *bidonvilles*. Omar had chosen the old imperial city of Meknes, where his father, his stepmother, a half sister, two half brothers, and a good number of his tribal cousins were already living. The city lies on a spur of a rolling barley-and-wheat plain called the Sais, southwest of Fez and just north of the foothills of the Middle Atlas, and it is only sixteen miles from the Jebel Zerhoun, Morocco's holy mountain, on which all of Omar's favorite saints are buried. Once, Meknes was a fortress for the early Ala-ouite Sultan Moulay Ismail. The Sultan was a sort of Ivan the Terrible of Morocco, and people in Meknes liked to say that he had harbored three great hopes in his heart when, in 1672, he put his slaves to work constructing his capital. First, Moulay Ismail hoped that the walls of his city, snaking for miles around the land that his seers and wise men had selected, would be the thickest, highest, mightiest walls in all Islam. Second, he hoped that his palace would be the most splendid and imposing palace ever to house a true descendant of the Prophet. And, third, he hoped that his dungeons, deep in the earth beneath the palace, would be the dankest, most alarming dungeons in which a Christian hostage, a Berber assassin, or a treacherous concubine would ever be put in screws.

Meknes turned out accordingly. The French soldiers who arrived at the city gates in 1911, at the vanguard of the protectorate, used the fortress to their own advantage, adding barracks and armories and drill fields, and eventually turning what had been a small *medina* of some thirty thousand Arabs into what was probably the largest French garrison in Africa, with twenty thousand permanently quartered troops. Then the *colons,* who came to Meknes next, put up a *ville nouvelle* on the site of the old royal olive groves, which had been levelled during a battle with the Berber tribesmen who still surrounded the city. The colonists' Meknes lay safely across a deep dry riverbed from the *medina* and the mad labyrinth of alleys that teemed with the native

Meknasiyyin. It had blocks of squat, diligently whitewashed houses, clipped hedges, potted bougainvilleas, and a little cement fountain, at the crossing of the two main *boulevardes,* that sprinkled colored water each Bastille Day. The *fellaha* came last, looking for day labor. They spread their vast *bidonvilles* over what were once the Sultan's fields and grazing grounds. By 1953, when Omar moved his family to the city, nearly a hundred and twenty thousand people were living in an ungainly conglomerate of *medina,* barracks, *bidonvilles,* and French provincial town. From the Sais plain, Meknes looked like a thread of bright, white light on the horizon; inside the city gates, it was heavy, gloomy, and oppressively flat. Squatters were keeping their chickens in Moulay Ismail's dungeons, there were shanties banked on his reflecting pools, and row on row of little clay-brick houses stood in the cool shadow of his walls.

Since 1962, Omar and his family had lived in one of these little brick houses. It was built, like the traditional Arab house, around a tiled courtyard, and it sat on the edge of a relatively new outlying quarter—most of it a *bidonville*—called Sidi Yussef, a few miles down a winding road from the tomb of a famous holy man who was called Sidi Lhadi ben Aissa but who preferred to go down in history as Sheikh el Kamel, or the Perfect Saint. (Moulay Ismail is also a saint

6

now, and he is revered by the Meknasiyyin, who expect him to use his persuasive powers on their behalf on Judgment Day.) The house cost Omar six thousand dirhams, or roughly twelve hundred dollars. He bought it with a check that came in the mail from France one day and that he took to be some sort of compensation for a year he had spent fighting Germans and Italians in the French Army. The French drafted Omar in 1941, when he was sixteen. He was sent to the Tunisian front, and he came home to his family with shrapnel in his side and a badly mangled right hand. Since then, much to his satisfaction, Omar had been unemployed. His settlement check, his fine new house with three rooms and a courtyard, and the monthly checks for two hundred and fifty dirhams that he had suddenly found himself receiving as a disabled *ancien combattant* of the French Republic were the envy of Sidi Yussef. Capital like Omar's was rare in the post-protectorate Moroccan kingdom, where most people got their wages daily, and where there was no reasonable credit system, either private or governmental, by which the poor—who were practically everyone—could borrow. His neighbors considered Omar, with his pension and his house, to be something of a man of means, but at the time I knew him, as it happened, he needed extra cash, because he wanted his own mule, too. Now, for most Moroccans who wanted to buy a mule, finance a circumcision feast, or start a business there were very few sure ways of raising money. One way, which was popular, was for the man of the family to take a stroll down the nearest highway and permit a car to run over him, trusting in Allah and the Prophet that he would live to collect his compensation from the driver's insurance company. Another way was to have a daughter, to guard her well, and, as early as nature and the law allowed, to give her in marriage, a certifiable virgin, to whoever bid the highest for her hand.

When I knew her, Khadija bint Omar was a gaunt, irritable adolescent with big yellow teeth and dirty hair. For the moment, she was also the most negotiable piece of property that Omar and Dawia had.

PART ONE

OMAR

Friday, June 16th: The sun was setting over the Jebel Zerhoun, and fifty thousand pilgrims to the mountain were pulling up their tent stakes and rolling their carpets, when Omar ben Allel announced to Allah, the Prophet, and all the saints of the land whose names he could remember that his daughter Khadija had disappeared. Omar was squatting in his own small tent, wrapped in a gray jellaba and desolately cracking a cone of sugar into a pot of mint tea. The

11

tent was pitched just off a footpath on the south face of the mountain, between the tombs of Sidi Ali ben Hamdush and Sidi Ahmed Dghughi, the two saints whose *musem*—yearly festival—the pilgrims had been celebrating, and from it Omar could hear Sidi Ahmed's followers singing and chattering as they led their burros down the path on the first leg of their journeys home. The pilgrims had travelled to the *musem* from the four corners of Morocco. Some of them had walked their burros, loaded with blankets and babies, and slung with pots and pans and clattering couscous platters, from as far to the south as Marrakech, Goulimine, and Essaouira, and one tiny tribe of Bedouins, anxious to cushion fate with a little of the saints' blessedness, had even come up out of the Sahara in a camel caravan. Omar himself was only twenty-five kilometres from his house in Sidi Yussef, but now that everybody else was leaving, he was eager to find his daughter before dark and head for home. There were always devils, demons, and assorted invisibles lurking about at night near holy places, and Omar was reluctant to go to sleep on a lonely mountain path with no other pilgrims around.

Dawia was sitting at the back of the tent, modestly enveloped in a ragged Cannon beach towel that had found its way to the *souks*—the markets —of Meknes in a batch of seconds from America. She had been wearing her towel for the last three

days. Her *hayk,* the long, shroudlike cloth with
which she generally protected herself, on trips,
against the inspection of strangers, had been
put in service as the right half of the family's
makeshift tent, and she had told her husband
earlier that she was looking forward to a change
of clothes. Dawia was a plump and handsome
woman of thirty-one with red, leathery cheeks,
long black braids, and a criss-crossing of blue
tattoos between her eyebrows, but all that was
visible of her at the moment was a hennaed hand,
a nipple, and one teary eye that had been rimmed
with kohl. She was nursing her latest baby, Jmaa,
and looking after four of her other children—
Abderrahman, Ali, Sidi Mohammed, and Saida.
Sidi Mohammed, who was six, was nibbling on a
date he had swiped from a little girl in a tent
down the footpath. His sister Saida, who was
four, was pouring holy water from a jug into a
couple of empty Coca-Cola bottles. And Ali and
Abderrahman, who were nine and ten and wanted
to be acrobats, were standing on their heads.
Omar's whole family was accounted for, except
Khadija, of course, and her older sister, Fatna,
who was a married woman of nearly eighteen.
Fatna was very modern, and she had no use for
saints and pilgrimages.

Omar had just returned from a grotto near
Sidi Ali's mausoleum where Aisha Qandisha,
the most terrible lady devil in Morocco, lived. A

13

few of the pilgrims were still in the grotto, paying their parting respects to Aisha with offerings of henna, black chickens, and scribbled verses from the Koran, and Omar had sat among them for an hour, hoping for a sign as to Khadija's whereabouts. He was on solid, intimate terms with Aisha Qandisha. She came to him in dreams, giving orders to follow and little bits of advice. Some of the neighbors, in fact, claimed that he was Aisha's lover, and they always laughed and said, "Aisha is jealous," when they heard that Omar had taken up the thick oak stick he kept in his house and beaten his children or his wife. Everyone knew by now that Aisha did not love Omar's missing daughter. She had struck Dawia with a madness on the day Khadija was born, and she had made the girl herself sullen and mysterious. Omar had searched for Khadija, who had been gone since morning, in four saints' tombs and a fair number of mountain villages, but he did not admit to Allah that his child was missing until he had visited Aisha's grotto and come back alone.

Dawia tucked her breast back into the folds of her towel, put Jmaa down, and stared sadly at her husband. He was a spindly, odd-looking man, tall for an Arab, with round, melancholy brown eyes, rotting teeth, and a bald scalp that was dappled here and there with iodine. Last year, at forty-one, conceding defeat to some ringworms that

14

Aisha sent him in a fit of jealousy, he had shaved his head.

Omar poured the mint tea, which had been steeping on a clay brazier, into two glasses on a small brass tray. Then he lifted one of the glasses, murmuring *"Bismillah"*—"In the name of Allah"—and pointing toward the path. The sun had set, and the pilgrims had started to light their way with torches and candles.

Dawia moaned for her daughter. "She has been struck by the devil—by *her*," she said. "It is certain."

"Perhaps she laughed at her father," Omar said, nodding.

"Perhaps she laughed at her mother, too," Dawia said.

Omar peered out at the slow procession of departing pilgrims. "We will wait until tomorrow morning," he said bravely. "Allah willing, I will have a dream tonight."

Saturday, June 17th: Omar had four half brothers. Two of them were shepherds and still lived in
the country. The other two, Mokhtar and Mustafa, were merchants of sorts, who travelled from
souk to *souk* across the Sais with trunks of stolen
clothes and contraband fabrics from Gibraltar,
and they lived near Omar in Sidi Yussef, with
their father, their mother, their wives, their
younger sister, and their assorted children, in a
small mud hut that was sided and roofed with
hammered-out tin cans. Their mother, Zahur, had

once been the second, subsidiary, wife in their
father's family, but she had been able to finish off
her predecessor, Omar's mother, with various
charms and magic potions, and now she devoted
herself entirely to preserving her husband's fortune—an armoire, three carpets, a round brass
tea tray, a silver-plated teapot, and some old
French francs sewn into a straw mattress—for
her own sons. For the past several years, she had
managed to keep her husband safely in the house,
where he occupied himself by praying all day
long in order to accumulate the good points he
would eventually need to get to Heaven.

Omar could hear his father praying this morning, when he knocked and waited politely at the
door to his brothers' hut. He had just come home
from the Jebel Zerhoun. He was wearing his best
clothes—a gray post-office uniform, which he had
owned since 1946, when he was arrested for taking a bite out of a neighbor during a dispute
over a stray sheep and sentenced by a French
contrôleur to four months as a janitor in the local
Bureau de Poste—and he was clean from a bath
in Sidi Ali's sacred spring. Mokhtar and Mustafa rarely bathed. Omar never saw them at the
hammam, which was the public steam bath, and
he often said to Dawia that the way to intimidate
his brothers was with the smell of soap.

Omar called out his name when his brothers,
inside, began to squabble loudly over who was at

18

their door. They had promised their sister, Zahara, to an old man from the *medina* who was
offering five thousand dirhams for a virgin under
sixteen, and, according to the old man's instructions, no stranger was to enter their hut until the
proper consummation of the marriage.

Finally, Mokhtar opened the door. He was a
stubby little man with bushy black hair and a
sweeping mustache, and he appeared invariably
in a torn undershirt and a pair of baggy green
trousers.

Mustafa came to the door behind him. He
looked a great deal like his brother, but his hair
was plastered down with water, his mustache was
oiled and glistening, and he was wearing a trim
gray suit and a tattersall vest. The clothes had
turned up recently, much to his delight, in a
package of smuggled acetate, and Mustafa had
appropriated them. He had a weakness for dancing girls, and despite his aversion to the *hammam,*
he always tried his best to be sporty and irresisti-
ble.

There was no light in the hut, because the old
man, whose name was Bushta, had ordered the
tiny courtyard boarded over to prevent competi-
tors from climbing onto the roof and staring
down at his fiancée. Omar had been there for several minutes before he saw that Bushta himself
was sitting next to him. Bushta, who was guarding Zahara for the morning, was peering sus-

piciously at Omar out of a pair of red-rimmed, astigmatic eyes. Last week, one of the neighbors had told him that Khadija was carrying messages from her Aunt Zahara to a handsome young melon merchant in the quarter, and Bushta suspected that the girl had not been duly punished for her treachery. Zahara herself had promptly been confined to a small, damp room across the courtyard, which the family used for sleeping and for storing grain. She was there now, hiding in a corner from her future husband, whom she had never actually met but whom she seemed to regard, according to her brothers, with an appropriately maidenly combination of terror and loathing. Her father, Allel, was praying in the room with her, and the various wives of the family, who were not permitted in the courtyard when the men had visitors, were huddled there around a brazier, making tea.

"Khadija has been struck," Omar told his brothers after he had drunk a guest's obligatory three glasses of mint tea.

Bushta looked up, pleased. He was a huge old man with greasy white whiskers and the smell of rancid olive oil on his jellaba.

"And now she has disappeared," Omar went on. "She left the tent to take a walk, on Friday morning . . ."

"Let us hope that all the virgins of the family are not in the habit of taking walks," Bushta said.

20

Zahara had spent two days at the *musem* with her brothers, and Bushta had not forgiven them.

"I am happy to say that our sister was always in the tent, under the eyes of her mother," Mustafa said quickly.

"She does not think of such things as taking walks," Mokhtar added, glaring at Omar.

"I am surprised that Khadija's father permitted her to take a walk," Bushta muttered.

"It was the devil who made her walk, not her father," Omar said, shaking his head sadly. Then he turned to his brothers. "I dreamed that *you* had seen her."

"The girl will come back," Mokhtar told him. "The daughter of our neighbor Ahmed was lost for a whole year. They found her begging at the Oujda *souk*."

"And then she died," Mustafa said cheerfully.

"That is what comes of taking walks," Bushta remarked.

Omar stood up to go. He embraced Mokhtar, who was chewing his thumb, and Mustafa, who was fiddling with the dial on a purple plastic transistor radio. Agadir was beating Kenitra at football.

"There is nothing in the world like football," Mustafa said.

Sunday, June 18th: This morning, after Omar
had his bread and coffee, he left his house and
walked up the alley to ask the advice of his neighbor Musa u Adja. Musa was a Berber from the
mountains near Marrakech. As a boy, he had
learned to read and write from a French soldier
who was stationed in his village, and now he
spoke not only Arabic, French, and three Berber
languages but a little Spanish, English, and
"American" as well. All the neighbors respected

23

him. He had the only library in Sidi Yussef—it consisted of a collection of every prisoner-of-war story that had appeared in *Paris Match* between 1960 and 1967, a copy of *Uncle Tom's Cabin* in colloquial French, and a finely illustrated manual of Arabian eroticism—and the most distinguished job. Musa earned five hundred dirhams a month as an interpreter for a young American who had come to Meknes to write a book about the Roman ruins near the Jebel Zerhoun. In keeping with his position, he had given away his jellaba, bought a pair of plaid trousers and a black turtleneck sweater, and announced that he was twenty-seven years old. Musa was forty, according to an old birth certificate, but twenty-seven was his favorite age.

Musa was in his courtyard with his wife, Habiba, when Omar knocked. Habiba was a dimpled, cross-eyed girl of nineteen with beautiful blue tattoos and a passion for beads and bracelets and the red, orange, and yellow dresses of her mountain tribe, and Musa was entirely satisfied with her. He had chosen her carefully. Her heels, according to his manual, were precisely the sort of heels that signified hot blood and great fertility in women. She had already given Musa two daughters, and at the moment she was pregnant again. This time, Musa was keeping her well draped with charms and amulets and scribbled verses from the Koran, which he hung on strings around her neck, tucked into the pockets of her bloomers, and pinned to the front of all her caftans. He wanted a son.

While Omar was settling down on a mat in Musa's courtyard, he remarked that the King had not come to the *musem,* as the blind seer who lived across the alley had predicted, and had therefore avoided spending a night in town in Moulay Ismail's drafty palace, where a company of the Royal Army had been observed putting the plumbing in order and mending chips in the mosaic tiles. Omar loved his King, he said, but he knew that whenever His Majesty Hassan II planned a visit to a city, his ministers would precede him, quickly constructing walls around the factories and the *bidonvilles.* There were already two such walls in Rabat, where the King usually lived. One of them went up in a single day, and it had brought much confusion to the workers who came home that night to find a long, high wall in the very place their neighborhood had been that morning. Omar and Musa were modest men. They knew that Sidi Yussef could be said to constitute a menace to the royal eyesight, and they had talked, before the *musem,* of Omar's returning to a "wall of shame."

"Perhaps he will not come to the *musem* at Moulay Idriss, either," Musa said, smiling. He was a skinny fellow with bright, black eyes and a pointed nose, and in his new black sweater he looked a little like a grounded crow.

"Or the festival of Moulay Ismail," Omar added.

"Still, a visit from the King would be a great honor," Musa said.

Omar looked at him. "I have come to the conclusion that Khadija was not struck by Aisha Qandisha," he said.

Musa leaned forward on his mat.

"She was stolen by Abdeslam ben Ali," Omar whispered. "I have had a dream about it all, and now I know."

Musa clucked sympathetically. He knew Abdeslam ben Ali well. Abdeslam was Bushta's tribal cousin, and he worked for the old man, driving a Volvo dump truck that Bushta had got hold of for a few hundred dirhams when a nervous French trucker fled the country in 1956, on Morocco's independence day. The Volvo was battered and rusty. It had been collapsing regularly for the past ten years, but Abdeslam still managed to see it through a weekly run from Meknes to Casablanca, transporting wares from merchants in the two cities to various *souks* along the route, and he was making his rich old cousin even richer than before. Sometimes he carried Mustafa, Mokhtar, and their fabrics in the truck with him. The men were friends, and, in fact, it

26

was Abdeslam who—out of his friendship for the brothers, and for a small consideration—had steered his cousin to Mustafa and Mokhtar when the old man first spoke of his desire to find a fresh young wife. Abdeslam himself had two wives, one in Casablanca and one in Meknes, as well as a woman along his route in the town of Khemisset.

"Ah, Abdeslam," Musa said, finally. "You know what they say about *him?* They say that when Abdeslam has a woman before his eyes, he cannot rest until he has taken her."

"It is that way with the blacks," Omar replied philosophically.

Musa nodded. He had great sympathy for Uncle Tom—Musa had read his book, weeping profusely, seven times since his American friend presented it to him—but the sympathy did not extend to black Moroccans. Black Moroccan tribes from the Sahara surrounded his mountain village every summer, taking the finest pastures for their starving sheep. Musa had been warned against them, just as his father had been warned, and his father's father, and all his ancestors. He had often observed that both Abdeslam and his cousin Bushta were the color of a sheep's liver, and he and Omar had had many long discussions of whether men the color of a sheep's liver were to be considered black or white. They agreed that Bushta was black, but until this morning

27

Omar had always maintained that his good friend
Abdeslam was very white.

"She was with Abdeslam the day before she
disappeared," Omar said.

"Ah," Musa replied, frowning.

"She was with him in the afternoon, and even
at night, after the sun set," Omar continued. "I
knew nothing. I was at Sidi Ahmed. I had heard
the music of my tribe, and it drew me. I danced.
I could not stop dancing—it had been a long time
since I had heard my proper *rih*."

"And then?" Musa interrupted. He knew that
Omar liked nothing better than talking about his
rih, which was the rhythm that drew him. Omar
was convinced that only the old drummers and
flutists of his scattered tribe could play his *rih*
correctly, and often, at night, he would keep his
neighbors up for hours, praising them.

"Then, when I had finished dancing, I returned to my tent," Omar said. "Do you know
what I found?"

"What did you find?" Musa asked him. "What
did you find?"

"I found Khadija, naturally," Omar said.

"Ah," Musa said.

"She had just come back," Omar went on.
"Her mother had called her uncles, in the next
tent, and she had confessed to her Uncle Mustafa
that she had driven alone with Abdeslam all the
way to the El Hajeb *souk*."

"Driving to El Hajeb takes a lot of gasoline," Musa remarked.

"Her Uncle Mustafa tied her up and beat her with my stick," Omar said.

"What a fine uncle," Musa said. "He thinks of the honor of his brother's family."

"No, no, no." Omar shook his head. "Mustafa thinks of the money he is getting for Zahara. He knows that if there is a scandal in the family, Bushta will take the part of his driver, and there will be no marriage."

"And abandon Zahara?" Musa broke in. "It is not possible." Word of Zahara's bride price had already reached him, and some of the neighbors were saying that Bushta, in his passion, had thrown in two sheep and a European mattress. Musa himself had got Habiba in the country for a hundred dirhams.

"Why not?" Omar said. "The driver is a cousin from his father's tribe."

"Still . . ." Musa said.

"And Abdeslam works for almost nothing," Omar added. "He does not even ask for a boy to do the loading."

"That is true," Musa said. "Most drivers ask for a boy."

"Bushta can always find a virgin," Omar said. "But where will he find another driver who works like that?"

"I will think on the problem," Musa promised.

"It is certain that Abdeslam came back to the mountain on Friday morning and stole my daughter—with the help of Aisha Qandisha," Omar said, walking to the door.

"You must ask him," Musa said.

Omar looked startled. "But that would be *hshuma*," he said. *Hshuma* was the word for "shame."

"You are right, that *would* be *hshuma*," Musa said quickly. He opened the door, and as soon as Omar left, he hurried down the alley to tell their neighbor the Widow Rabha the news.

Monday, June 19th: This morning, Omar told
Dawia that he was of many minds on the subject
of their daughter. Now that she had been stolen,
he said, he could not help thinking that perhaps
she should stay stolen forever and spare him a
reconciliation which would bring great *hshuma* to
everyone. Still, yesterday the blind seer claimed
to have "seen" Khadija in a white hut near a
lemon tree somewhere to the south of the city,
and *he* was insisting that it was Allah's will that
Omar go looking for her there. (Like most of the
men in Sidi Yussef, Omar often said that the

seer, the *shuwwaf,* had no power—"If he is blind, tell me, how can he see?" Omar would ask whenever Dawia slipped a dirham from the mint money into her pocket and paid the seer a visit—but already, since Khadija's disappearance, he had sent Dawia down the road for a consultation five times.) And Musa, for his part, wanted to overlook the will of Allah for the moment and report the black abductor Abdeslam ben Ali to the police.

Finally, Omar came to the conclusion that he could not abandon Khadija entirely. Dawia had been refusing food as a mark of grief, and Sidi Mohammed had been bawling all morning for his sister, who had always been next to him at night on the family's sleeping carpet. Omar told Dawia that he was going to stop at the Commissariat of Police—after all, he was a man who could deal with policemen—and that then he would borrow Mokhtar's and Mustafa's mule and head south. Leaving her with another dirham for the *shuwwaf,* who had promised them a fresh vision by lunchtime, he put the family *hala madaniyya* in an old leather pouch—a *hala madaniyya* was an official family-status declaration and nobody could do business with the government without one—and started walking toward the center of the *ville ancienne.*

The Commissariat in the *medina* was a gloomy concrete compound with a dusty courtyard, and its only distinction lay in the fact that it stood beside the Bab Mansour, Moulay Ismail's most imposing city gate. When Omar walked in, a group of black-booted policemen were standing around the courtyard, playing with their pistols and arguing loudly. For a while, none of them noticed the tall, bald man in the French post-office uniform who waited by the door, at a respectful distance, and smoked his way through a pocketful of cigarette butts. They were discussing the merits of James Bond's laser gun, which they had all seen yesterday at the movies for the first time.

Finally, Omar approached them, with his last butt burning between the fingers of his left hand. "My daughter has been stolen," he said.

The policemen shrugged. One of them asked for Omar's *hala madaniyya,* flipped through the torn gray folder, and tossed it back to Omar, frowning. He had seen that Omar lived in Sidi Yussef, and was not likely to have relatives in the government. "Why do you bother us with these things?" he said. "We have important work to do here."

"She has been gone since Friday," Omar said.

"Come back tomorrow or next week," the policeman said, turning away. "We are very busy."

Omar waited until another policeman spoke to him.

"How can I help you?" the second policeman asked politely, folding his hands across his belly. His belly was enormous.

Omar smiled. He knew that policemen who wanted to stay as fat and as healthy as the one in front of him usually took bribes—bakshish—to pay their debts at the sugar *souk,* and were bound to be more agreeable than the strict, thin ones. "She was stolen by a truck driver during the *musem* of Sidi Ahmed Dghughi," he told the fat policeman.

The policeman looked at Omar's *hala madaniyya.* "That is to say, she was stolen on the mountain," the policeman said.

"Exactly," Omar replied.

"Then, my friend, you must know that the mountain is not in the jurisdiction of the Commissariat," the policeman said. "Only the city belongs to the Commissariat. Crimes committed in the country belong to the Gendarmerie Royale."

"My daughter *lives* in the city," Omar said.

"But she was stolen in the country, was she not?" the policeman asked.

Omar nodded.

"So it is up to Gendarmerie to find her," the policeman said.

"The driver also lives in the city," Omar cut in.

The policeman shook his head. Omar, he said, would have to travel, at great expense, to the Gendarmerie Royale in the town of Moulay Idriss, on the Jebel Zerhoun.

Omar tapped his leather pouch and listened to the dirhams jingling inside it. Then he looked up bashfully and grinned. The policeman grinned at Omar. In a minute, Omar and the policeman were shaking hands in a little office off the court-yard.

"All told, it will be a great saving," the police-man whispered, nodding in the direction of a big black telephone on a desk in the middle of the room. Then he called to a guard who was stand-ing at attention in a corner, and told him to phone the Gendarmerie at Moulay Idriss right away.

The guard marched up to the telephone and began to dial with slow, elaborate flourishes. He stopped suddenly. "You are not permitted to call the Gendarmerie!" he shouted, slamming down the receiver.

"And why is that?" the policeman asked him.

"The telephone is only for official business"—the guard reached into the top drawer of the desk, pulled out a sheet of paper, and waved it around —"and, as you can see, the Gendarmerie is not on the official-business list."

"But my daughter has been stolen on the Jebel Zerhoun," Omar began again.

"Surely that is not *my* affair," the guard broke in.

"You will telephone the Gendarmerie," the po-liceman ordered.

"There can be no question of telephoning the Gendarmerie," the guard said. "It is not listed on the budget."

The fat policeman started jumping up and
down. Omar walked softly out of the room, so
that his new friend would not lose face in front
of him. He waited by the door, but after ten
minutes the policeman and the guard were still
screaming at each other, so he left the Commissariat and walked home.

Tuesday, June 20th: Omar rode out of the city on his brothers' mule this morning, stopping to ask about Khadija at villages with whitewashed huts and lemon trees. He travelled for several hours, and then, riding home alone toward late afternoon, he overtook Musa on the Sidi Yussef road. Musa was walking down the road with a tin of Bulgarian apricot jam tucked under his arm. Habiba, he explained, had developed a strange and often implacable craving for this rare preserve, which she had tasted once at the American's house. Only this morning, she had refused

37

to make his bread or sift the couscous until he promised her a new tin. He had just spent two hours in the *medina* bargaining down the price with a sugar-and-jam merchant, and a third hour at the home of a certain *fqih*—a scholar of the Koran who could work powerful magic with the Koranic texts and who was famous throughout Meknes as a specialist in pregnant women. The *fqih* had instructed Musa to burn two spices and a short verse from the Koran in a new brazier. Musa's marriage would then be safe from further extravagant expenses, and his wife would be relatively docile and obedient until their son was born.

Omar knew the *fqih*. Once, in a similar emergency, he had used the man himself. Musa, jogging along beside the mule, was encouraged to hear that Dawia had not demanded anything out of the ordinary since 1962.

"I have not found the girl," Omar said after the men had travelled for a while in silence. "I have been looking all day."

Musa shook his head sadly.

"I have been in every village from here to Boufekrane looking for the girl," Omar went on. He did not like to use his daughter's name, now that she had been stolen and had disgraced him.

"It has been only five days," Musa said. "Allah willing, she will still be a virgin when we find her."

38

"For thirteen years I have bought her food,"
Omar began, ignoring him. "I have bought her
clothes. I have even sent her to school. And now
they say I am to pay five dirhams for a taxi to
Moulay Idriss." Omar sighed. "Five dirhams—
it is not worth it," he said.

Musa remarked that every tin of apricot jam
cost *him* four and a half dirhams. "Allah gives
problems to us all," he said.

"And now who will ask for her in marriage?"
Omar continued. "No one will give me a single
dirham for her. I will have to lock her in the house
when we find her. I will have to hire a guard to
watch her. I will be feeding her until I die."
Omar shrugged helplessly. "Five dirhams to go
to Moulay Idriss, and that is just the beginning.
No, it is not worth it. I will forget her."

The men had come to Omar's house, and Omar
slid off his brothers' mule and opened the door.
He saw Dawia, lying on a mat in the middle of
the courtyard, surrounded by seven old women
from the neighborhood. Six of the women were
sobbing loudly. The seventh woman, who was the
oldest and ugliest of them all, was telling them a
story about a ravished innocent.

Omar shut the door immediately. "I am going
to Moulay Idriss after all," he said.

Wednesday, June 21st: Tonight, when the muezzin climbed to the roof of the little mosque in Sidi Yussef to chant the last call to prayer until tomorrow morning, Omar was hiding behind a pile of garbage just across a muddy alley from the wattle-and-daub hut that belonged to Abdeslam's Meknes wife. Although it was *hshuma* to do so, Omar had made up his mind to ask the driver for his daughter, and, from his post behind the garbage, he was listening for the sound of the dump truck, returning to Sidi Yussef from its tour of the country *souks*.

41

Omar had had a busy, wearying day. He and
Musa had ridden up to Moulay Idriss in a taxi;
he had prayed at the tombs of three saints in the
medina; he had been to the mosque in Sidi Yussef; and he had scoured the quarter for witnesses
against his treacherous friend. He had found one
witness at a little coffeehouse where the *anciens
combattants* from the neighborhood met in the
afternoon to play cards. This witness had never
met Khadija—in fact, he had never met Abdeslam ben Ali either—but he said to Omar, to
whom he owed ten dirhams, "I have confidence in
you, my friend, and whatever I hear from your
lips I am going to say before the *gendarmes.*"
Omar had less luck finding other witnesses. Mustafa and Mokhtar refused him; they had just received their new mattress from Bushta, and
Abdeslam himself had been coming to their house
all week with kilo sugar cones. Zahara had also
refused, after her brothers announced that they
would hang her from the ceiling by her eyelids if
she did anything to cool the ardor and close the
purse of her fiancé. And two truck drivers who
claimed to have seen Khadija and Abdeslam together last Thursday in El Hajeb refused, on the
ground that Abdeslam might then be inclined to
testify against *them* if they should ever have the
good fortune to make off with a young girl.

It was now nearly eleven o'clock, and Omar
had been hiding behind the garbage since eight,

when he left the truck drivers. He had a cramp
in his foot. He was shivering in his thin jellaba.
(They were saying in Sidi Yussef that the nights
were cool this summer because of all the "sput-
niks" the Americans had been hanging in the sky
on their way to the moon.) And he was worried
about invisibles, who were known to frequent
garbage pails. He wanted to go home, but he had
promised Dawia that he would see the driver. The
shuwwaf had advised a meeting with Abdeslam
tonight.

Omar was looking up at the sky, trying to tell
the satellites from the stars, when he heard the
roar of a broken exhaust pipe. In a moment, Abdeslam's truck came rattling down the alley,
scraping against the huts and raising huge clouds
of dust and smoke. It stopped just short of the
garbage, and Abdeslam climbed out, singing to
himself. Omar noticed that tonight he was even
darker than a sheep's liver. His cheeks were hol-
low and his ears stuck out. Still, he was tall and
straight, and he had a fine, thick mustache. All
things considered, Abdeslam was a rather handsome man.

Omar took one step out from behind the garbage. Then he stopped, peered at the old wristwatch he was wearing, and stepped back into the
dark with a sigh of relief. It was eleven-thirty—
much too late for a gentleman to go visiting.

Thursday, June 22nd: In Sidi Yussef, where the Islam was very definitely not the Islam of Koranic scholars, it was generally agreed that there were four kinds of human beings in the universe —Muslims, Jews, pagans, and Europeans. Muslims were the true believers, and any Muslim with enough good points to his spiritual credit on Judgment Day would get to Heaven eventually. Jews and pagans would never get to Heaven, with the exception of Sidina Musa, or Moses, who had a close working arrangement with Allah. But

45

Europeans had been blessed with a certain option
as to whether they would get to Heaven or not.
(In Arabic, the word for a European was *nesrani*
—Christian—and no one in Sidi Yussef would
consider the possibility that there were Christians
who were not Europeans or Europeans who were
not Christians.) A European who repented the
error of his faith and proclaimed the *shahada*—
"There is but one God and Mohammed is His
Prophet"—before dying would always go directly to Heaven, no matter what his spiritual
standing. Dawia maintained that the Europeans
were thus favored by Allah because Allah liked
automobiles and was hoping that the Europeans
would bring their cars to Heaven with them.
Omar, however, said no, that Allah loved the Europeans because the Europeans always got to
their appointments on time.

Omar had known many Frenchmen in the
Army, but Musa's patron was the first American
nesrani he had ever met. They had been friends
for a year—ever since the night Dawia was lamed
in her left foot by a blue, uncircumcised devil,
whom she had offended by sifting semolina over a
drain in the courtyard that the devil inhabited,
and Omar was obliged to call in a group of Sidi
Ahmed's followers to play her *rih* on their reed
flutes. Dawia had danced to her *rih* and been
cured quite early in the evening—she had a
couscous to prepare for all the company and

could not afford much time for getting better—
but the same blue devil had also been giving
Omar trouble that week, and later in the evening
Omar himself had started dancing. He was leaping up and down, deep in trance, when Musa,
who had been invited to the cure along with forty
or fifty of the neighbors, dropped by with the
American. The American had been very much
impressed with the way Omar soothed the devil.
He began driving out to Sidi Yussef, and by now
he had spent many happy afternoons in Omar's
courtyard listening to his new friend's stories.

At six-thirty this morning, Omar knocked at
the American's door in the *ville nouvelle,* where
there were still three movie theatres, six pharma-
cies, a tennis-racquet merchant, and a few thousand Europeans left over from the protectorate.
Musa was with Omar, looking extremely tired.
He had been up since four, when Omar had run
down the alley to report on a new dream, in which
he had been instructed by Sidi Ahmed himself to
ask for help from the American. Omar had
wanted to leave at once, but Musa had managed
to keep him in Sidi Yussef, drinking coffee, until
now.

The American opened the door, yawning. He
was wearing a plaid bathrobe. "My God, Musa,
it's six-thirty in the morning," he said.

"Praise be to Allah that it is not four in the
morning," Musa said, shaking hands.

Omar also shook hands with the American. He inquired politely about the American's health, the health of his wife, the health of his paternal relatives in the city of Sneden's Landing, New York, the success of his work, and his opinion of the weather of the past few days. He called the American "Monsieur Hugh," because he had never mastered the pronunciation of his friend's last name.

Monsieur Hugh, who was still yawning, showed his guests into his living room. He was a young man with blue eyes, like a Rifian Berber's, and brown hair that curled down over the collar of his robe. The fact that Monsieur Hugh's hair was longer than the hair of Monsieur Hugh's wife had always puzzled Omar, but Musa claimed that this was the custom in America.

When Monsieur Hugh, in turn, had asked about Omar's health, the health of Omar's wife, the health of each of Omar's children, and the health of his paternal relatives, the men sat down together on a couch with red cushions, and Omar began to talk about his missing daughter. He knew that Musa had already told his boss the story, but it would have been *hshuma* to acknowledge this.

"And so, yesterday, we went by taxi to the Gendarmerie Royale at Moulay Idriss," Musa said when Omar had come to his telephone problems at the Commissariat.

"And what did *they* say?" Monsieur Hugh
asked.

"They said that the Commissariat belongs to
the Minister of the Interior and that the Gendarmerie belongs to the General of the Maison
Militaire Royale," Musa said. "And that the
Commissariat policemen are not permitted to
telephone the gendarmes, but that, thanks to the
wisdom and generosity of their general, the gendarmes, in emergencies, are permitted to telephone the policemen."

"I meant about Khadija," Monsieur Hugh
said.

"The gendarme at the door said that a woman
of thirteen is old enough to take care of herself,"
Musa said.

"That's ridiculous," Monsieur Hugh interrupted. "Khadija's a child."

"No," Omar said sadly. "Her mother was married, and with a baby, at her age."

"And so the gendarme told us to go away,"
Musa continued. "But at that moment his chief
walked in."

"He said to Musa, 'Ah, haven't I seen you in
Meknes in the American's automobile?'" Omar
said.

"And he invited us into his office," Musa
added. "He said that his name was Abdelazziz
ben Abdelqader, but that we could call him Monsieur le Chef de Gendarmerie."

"It was a splendid office," Omar said. "It was very, very big. And there were many papers on the desk."

"He looked at his papers for a long time," Musa said. "And then he breathed very loudly" —Musa huffed and puffed—"to show us what a busy man he was."

"And *then* he spoke to the caid of Moulay Idriss on his telephone," Omar said.

"About Khadija?" Monsieur Hugh asked.

"Oh, no," Omar said. "He spoke to the caid about the caid's bicycle, which was stolen at the *musem* the same day that my daughter was stolen. He told the caid that all the gendarmes were very busy looking for it."

"And then he asked us many questions," Musa said proudly.

"He asked for a description of Khadija?" Monsieur Hugh said.

"No," said Omar.

"Did he ask for her picture?" Monsieur Hugh said.

"Oh, no." Omar shook his head.

"He asked us how much you had to pay for your blue Opel," Musa announced. "He said that your Opel is very beautiful, but that he, personally, prefers a Mercedes-Benz."

"He also asked us where you bought your automobile," Omar cut in.

"And then he asked for your address," Musa

said. "He told us that he is coming to the *ville nouvelle* very soon to talk with you about automobiles. He says that he is an expert on all the automobiles of Europe but that he would like some information on the automobiles the Americans make."

"This is incredible," Monsieur Hugh said to his wife, who had just awakened and was walking through the living room, in her own plaid bathrobe, on her way to the kitchen. Madame Hugh, as she was called in Sidi Yussef, was a small, blond woman without much fat on her. Once, Omar had suggested that Monsieur Hugh lock her in the house for a month or two and feed her dates and sugar cones, as any Moroccan with a scrawny wife would do, but Musa had told him that not only was Madame Hugh extremely happy to be scrawny but Monsieur Hugh actually preferred her that way. Omar had not believed Musa. He had said that the woman was obviously putting aside the marketing money, in the event that Monsieur Hugh abandoned her for a second wife when she got old.

Madame Hugh came back with coffee for the men, and sat down on the couch, next to Omar. "And how is Dawia?" she asked when she had heard his story.

"She cries all day, and my house is full of women who drink my tea and eat my children's food," Omar complained. "And when she is not listening to the women, she is listening to the *shuwwaf*."

"And what does the *shuwwaf* suggest?" Madame Hugh asked.

"Yesterday morning, he said that the girl was in a white hut, south of the city," Omar told her. "But later he said that she was *in* the city, locked in the house of a woman named Malika."

"I'm taking Omar to the Commissariat to swear out a complaint against the truck driver," Monsieur Hugh said.

"And then, early this morning, the *shuwwaf* said that Dawia was to burn three verses of the Koran," Omar continued. "He said that the odor of the Koran burning would surely draw the girl back to her own home."

"What if the door's locked—wherever she is?" Monsieur Hugh broke in.

"She will escape, even if the door is locked," Omar said. "Perhaps the door is made out of old wood or—"

"But perhaps the door is made out of iron," Musa said.

"Even if the door is *iron,* she will escape," Omar told him.

"Perhaps what the *shuwwaf* really meant to say was that through the power of the Koran the *police* would be able to break the door down," Madame Hugh suggested.

"That is very intelligent for a woman," Musa said, admiringly.

Omar thought for a minute, and then he said, "You are right. Monsieur Hugh will get the police, and the police will break the door down, and then exactly what the *shuwwaf* has said will come to pass."

Madame Hugh nodded. "We must attack the problem from all directions," she said. "Allah would not have made policemen unless He wanted us to use them, for emergencies."

"That is true," Musa said.

Madame Hugh sat back, looking pleased with herself. She went on talking about policemen while her husband was in their bedroom, getting dressed. Then, when the men climbed into the blue Opel, which was parked at the curb beyond her flowering-cactus patch, she called to Omar from the door to remember what she had said. Omar, however, was busy trying to explain to Monsieur Hugh that girls stolen in the country did not belong to the Commissariat.

Monsieur Hugh did not believe him and headed for the Commissariat office in the *ville nouvelle*.

"You'd better tell me everything," Monsieur Hugh said. "You're sure it was the driver?"

"I am sure," Omar said.

"That is to say, he is sure, but not *precisely* sure," Musa told him. "The driver admits that he was with the girl on Thursday, in El Hajeb, but he has sworn by the saint of Omar's village that he has not seen her since then."

"He swore that?" Monsieur Hugh asked Omar. "To you?"

"Oh, no," Omar said. "He swore to my brother Mustafa when they were drinking tea together."

"Haven't you seen him?" Monsieur Hugh looked incredulous. "I thought he had a wife near you in Sidi Yussef."

"That is so," Omar said.

"Look," Monsieur Hugh said, pulling up in front of a big building across the street from an Esso station with an Arabic "Put a Tiger in Your Tank" sign. "What did Khadija say on Thursday after your brother beat her? Did she say she was—um—raped?"

"There were ten dirhams in her pocket," Musa said.

"But she would not tell her mother why Abdeslam had given them to her," Omar added. "And so her mother said, 'Well, then, you will have to be examined by someone who knows about such things.'"

"It is not wise to say that if you are in a tent and have no means of locking up the girl afterward," Musa remarked.

Monsieur Hugh sighed, rolled up his car windows, and urged Omar and Musa through the Commissariat door. Ten minutes later, they were back in the Opel. They had had an instructive conversation with the head of the Service de Mineurs about whether Khadija was a child, as

54

Monsieur Hugh insisted, or a woman, as the policeman claimed. While they were debating the question, the policeman thought to look at the address in Omar's *hala madaniyya*. Then he sent them back to the *medina* Commissariat.

It was eight-thirty by the time the men arrived at the *medina,* but most of the Commissariat there was still closed. Eventually, they found a policeman in a back office called the Service de Résidence.

"How old is the girl?" the policeman asked after Monsieur Hugh told him that Khadija was missing.

"Thirteen," Omar said.

"Thirteen?" the policeman repeated. "So she is *old*. She can look out for herself."

"That is what everybody says," Musa volunteered.

Omar flipped through his *hala madaniyya* and pointed to a snapshot of Khadija that was glued to the back page.

The policeman looked it over. "She could be fourteen, even fifteen," he said.

"We want to make a complaint against the man who stole her," Omar told him. "We have a witness."

"Then you will have to go to Moulay Idriss," the policeman said.

Omar glanced at Monsieur Hugh and grinned.

"This man has *been* to Moulay Idriss," Monsieur Hugh said. "And, furthermore, he lives *here,* in Sidi Yussef. And the man who stole his daughter lives in Sidi Yussef. One would think—"

"Who is this man?" the policeman demanded, pointing at Monsieur Hugh. "He is a lawyer! Do not try to deny that he is a lawyer!"

"He is my friend," Omar said weakly.

The policeman had grabbed the sleeve of Omar's jellaba and was tugging at it. "Why did you bring him, then?" the policeman asked him. "It is *hshuma!*" He waved toward the door. "Go away," he said. "Go to Moulay Idriss."

"Moulay Idriss is forty kilometres from here," Monsieur Hugh said. "He cannot afford to keep going to Moulay Idriss."

The policeman shrugged. "Then there is nothing to be done," he said.

"Don't you understand?" Monsieur Hugh shouted. "This man's child is missing!"

The policeman shrugged again. "She is old enough to take care of herself," he said.

"Listen to me," Monsieur Hugh told the policeman. "This man is a human being. He is suffering. His family is suffering. His daughter may be dead."

"Do you suggest that there are murders in my district?" the policeman asked Monsieur Hugh.

Omar and Musa started backing toward the door. Omar had taken off the turban he was wearing and was blotting the sweat on his head with his *hala madaniyya*.

"It will do you no good to go to Moulay Idriss anyway," the policeman said, turning his back on them. "No one can make a complaint without the signature of two witnesses."

"Europeans," Omar whispered to Musa when Monsieur Hugh lost his temper and began hollering. "They are very just, but what do they understand?"

PART
TWO

DAWIA

Wednesday, July 5th: Early this afternoon, while the children played hopscotch in the alley, Dawia was squatting on her heels before the blind *shuwwaf,* listening to the seer sniff loudly at the spices burning in his clay brazier and tap the floor with the fingers of his right hand. This was the way the *shuwwaf* saw. He was dressed in a black jellaba, out of respect for Aisha Qandisha, who had given him his special sight in exchange for the sight with which he used to look at mortal women. The walls of his little hut were also black.

61

There were no candles. One of the seven old women, who had come with Dawia for the latest news about Khadija, kept muttering to the others, "It is not only the *shuwwaf* who has difficulty seeing in the *shuwwaf's* house."

Twenty days had passed now since Khadija disappeared. This morning, when the *shuwwaf* tapped his floor, he had seen her locked in a damp room somewhere in a village called El Haj Kaddour; he had a new message from Aisha this afternoon. "The girl is in Meknes again," he said after he had stopped tapping. "She has forgotten her family"—Dawia groaned softly—"and she is wearing a gray caftan. A woman guards her. She is in a place"—the *shuwwaf* tapped again—"a place where there are thieves. I see trees. Many trees."

The old women, huddled against a wall, nodded contentedly and whispered to one another that the *shuwwaf* rarely went into such detail for a customer. Dawia pressed a dirham into the *shuwwaf's* palm. The old man, who had been able to lay in spices for the next three months with the money Dawia had given him already, hoisted the hem of his jellaba and deposited the coin in a leather pouch that was hanging from his baggy trousers. Then he held out his hand again, and Dawia kissed it.

"Remember the trees," the *shuwwaf* said.

Dawia nodded. There were woods in Meknes

that ran through a deep ravine along the road
from the *medina* out to Sidi Yussef, and they
were called Suhi, after an old thief who had hidden there from the sultan's soldiers centuries ago.
By now there was not a thief in the city who at
one time or another had not waited out a man-
hunt in one of the tiny huts that Suhi's cousins
and sons and grandsons, all of whom followed
Suhi's profession, had built in the old man's
woods. Suhi was dense and dark, and everybody
in Meknes said that it was very dangerous. Even
Lieutenant Brahim, the head of the criminal bri-
gade at the Gendarmerie Royale, refused to go
there. Last week, after Monsieur Hugh met
Brahim at the Esso station and established the
binding fact that they had both shared tea with
the pasha's chief assistant, the Lieutenant had set
out three times to search Suhi for Khadija. The
first time, he had turned back for his dress uniform. The second time, he had turned back for an
extra pistol. And the third time, he had turned
back for no reason at all. According to Musa,
who had gone with him, the Lieutenant had said,
"You know, it is really too dangerous for me
down there."

Dawia, trailed by the old women, hurried to her
house to report to Omar. She found him on the
roof. Mustafa was with him, and they were listening to Musa read a letter that Mokhtar, who had
been out of town all week at the *souk* in Sidi

Kacem, had just sent home on a passing milk truck. Musa was in great demand as a letter reader. He read with drama and solemnity, as befitted the written word, and, furthermore, he charged nothing for his services.

"So, you see, it is not Abdeslam after all," Mustafa said when Musa had finished his third, and best, rendition of the letter.

"Abdeslam is a good man," Omar said. "I have always said so."

"Abdeslam has eaten with us all," Musa added.

"Haven't I always said that Abdeslam is a good man?" Omar asked Dawia.

Dawia began to cry. "What has happened to my daughter?" she said.

"Didn't Abdeslam swear by our saint that he would never do such a terrible thing?" Mustafa asked Omar.

"Where is my daughter?" Dawia said.

"You are certainly lucky to have a brother who can write letters," Mustafa went on.

Musa scrutinized the letter. "All told, it is not a bad letter," he said.

Dawia pulled at her husband's hand. "Where is my daughter?" she pleaded.

"Ah, the girl," Omar said, looking surprised. "Mokhtar has heard at the *souk* that she is the prisoner of a man from Sidi Kacem." Then he turned to Musa. "*You* have heard me say that Abdeslam is a good man, haven't you?"

"And you are lucky to have brothers who know the *souks,* who hear things," Mustafa cut in. He was jumping around, excited, and he told Musa that very, very soon, Allah willing, Musa would have an invitation to Zahara's wedding. Lately, Bushta had been putting the wedding off. He had told Mustafa and Mokhtar that he was waiting to see the good name of his driver restored, but the brothers suspected that he had been listening to the gossip of jealous mothers in the quarter. The mothers were saying that Zahara was brazen. Once, they said, she had even joined the Girl Scouts.

"You will go to Sidi Kacem?" Dawia demanded. She tugged at Omar. "You will find my daughter?"

Omar thought for a minute. "Perhaps we will just leave her in Sidi Kacem," he said.

Mustafa nodded enthusiastically. He said that he himself had been about to suggest leaving Khadija in Sidi Kacem.

Musa glared at them both. He had been talking to Monsieur Hugh about stolen women and had come to the conclusion that is was not altogether civilized to abandon them. "What if she is still a virgin?" he asked. "You will be throwing away a good bride price."

"We will go to Sidi Kacem," Omar said.

"The trip to Sidi Kacem is not cheap," Mustafa said. "I, for one—"

"But we will ask our good friend Abdeslam ben Ali to drive us to Sidi Kacem in the dump truck," Omar said.

Thursday, July 6th: Just as the *shuwwaf*'s hut
was painted black, the three small rooms that
opened off the courtyard of Omar's house were
painted according to the preferences of the devils
to whom the family was particularly close. The
tiny kitchen, where Dawia kept her brazier, her
charcoal, and her sacks of semolina, was yellow,
in honor of a lady devil by the name of Lalla
Mira. The *bit dyaf*—the "room of the guests"
—where Omar served mint tea to his company,
was blue, in honor of another lady devil, Lalla

67

Malika. And the room where the family ate and slept was blood red, in honor of Aisha, who was said to consider the color a worthy substitute for the black she loved.

Dawia spent this morning in the red room, intermittently nursing Jmaa and listening to her eldest daughter, Fatna, sniffle into a straw pillow and complain about everything. Fatna was a big, pretty girl who went to football matches with her husband and had been seen by the neighbors out walking in a short skirt. She had bright, greedy eyes and a voice that could be soft and coaxing when she was not crying or complaining. It was rumored that she shaved her legs.

Fatna did not like coming home. She liked the *medina,* where she lived with her husband and his parents, and she liked the *ville nouvelle,* where she went to stenographers' school, but, as she often told her mother, she was ashamed of Sidi Yussef. She had arrived last night, just after Omar and Mustafa left for Sidi Kacem in Abdeslam's truck. All night long, she had wept on Dawia's stomach, and already this morning she had walloped Saida and thrown her shoes at Abderrahman. Everyone knew why she was angry: Fatna had had a fight with her mother-in-law.

Fatna's husband was a young male nurse named Driss, and people in Sidi Yussef who had been to the movies said that he was as handsome as Omar Sharif. He worked at the Sidi Said

Hospital, on the road to Rabat, which was one
of the largest public hospitals in Morocco. It was
also one of the most rewarding. All the nurses at
Sidi Said were bakshish rich. Driss earned his
own particular bakshish by selling permissions
to see the doctor to the patients on the critical
ward and, afterward, by selling them the medi-
cines that the doctor prescribed. Shots of penicillin, which people in Meknes considered very
potent European magic, brought the best prices
at the hospital, and around the *medina,* where
Driss had established himself as a "Doctor of
Operations," there were hundreds of merchants
who would buy whatever shots his hospital patients could not afford. Driss always kept his
cache of penicillin and syringes sealed in a tin
box next to his mattress in the family bedroom.
But last night, when he came home from the
hospital, the box was open, the syringes shat-
tered, and there were puddles of penicillin all
over the floor. Fatna had said that her mother-in-
law dropped the box that morning. Her mother-
in-law told Driss that Fatna dropped the box
herself. Driss had sided with his mother in the
fight that followed—it was great *hshuma,* in such
a situation, to take the part of one's wife—and
Fatna had left the house, wearing her three best
caftans under her jellaba and clutching a tube
of purple lipstick, and hailed a taxicab to Sidi
Yussef.

Dawia listened to Fatna's moans and sniffles till noon, when Musa stopped by with Madame Hugh. Musa was to have gone with the other men to Sidi Kacem, but he had had to cancel his trip at the last moment, because Habiba had developed a craving for freshly slaughtered goat. Despite his domestic troubles, Musa was relieved to have avoided the dangerous mission to Sidi Kacem. He had been cheerful all day.

"Why are you moaning like that?" Madame Hugh asked Fatna after they had kissed on both cheeks, according to the French fashion, which Fatna was cultivating. Madame Hugh sounded impatient. She had been angry with Fatna since the day she heard Fatna tell her little brothers that soldiers were coming all the way from Israel to Sidi Yussef to eat them up. Fatna had learned about the soldiers from Driss, who had a short-wave radio and liked to listen to the news on Radio Cairo at night, just before the world football scoreboard.

"Fatna has fought with her mother-in-law again," Dawia explained. Then she got up to find a towel for her guest's bare knees; Fatna was staring wistfully at the American's miniskirt.

Madame Hugh spread the towel carefully. One day last week, she had driven Dawia up and down a street of brothels in the *medina,* looking for Khadija, and Dawia had crouched for shame on the floor of the car. Madame Hugh had told her not to be shamed by the prostitutes, but Dawia had replied that she was not shamed by the prostitutes—she was shamed by Madame Hugh's short skirt.

"It is all because of Khadija," Fatna said, between her sniffles. "She has disgraced her family, and it is because of *her* that my mother-in-law dropped the penicillin. So that Driss will be angry and divorce me."

"Fatna is waiting for her mother-in-law to come with a gift and apologize," Dawia told Madame Hugh.

"She has already sent Driss, but that is not enough," Fatna said. "I will not go back until she comes for me herself."

"It is a burden to have daughters," Dawia said, sighing. "My husband looks at Jmaa now and he says, 'What can I expect from her? More of the same problems I have suffered with the first two.'"

"He has a point," Musa remarked. "Having daughters is not profitable."

"My father thinks of nothing but the money he will get for his daughters," Fatna cut in. She was referring to the matter of her *sdaq*—her bride price. Just before her wedding, Driss had heard from a doctor at the hospital that in Europe husbands and wives shared all of their expenses, so he had refused to sign the marriage papers until it was agreed that Fatna would pay

half of her own bride price to Omar. At first,
Omar had torn up the papers and sworn that
Driss would never enter his house again, but
Fatna had already been seen by the neighbors in
Driss's company, and in the end there was nothing for Omar to do but accept the terms. Then,
too, Fatna was nearly seventeen, and it had
seemed unlikely to Omar that another man would
ever want her. After much bargaining, the marriage act had been stamped and sealed by the
judge at the marriage court. Driss had promised
two hundred and fifty dirhams as a down payment, and Fatna was to give her father two
hundred and fifty dirhams more, in monthly in-
stallments, as soon as she finished stenographers'
school and got a job. The judge, who was an old
man in a red fez, had told Omar this was the
strangest marriage act that he had ever witnessed.
Omar had been ashamed—he himself had paid a
good, respectable *sdaq* to Dawia's father, he had
given many presents to her family, and he had
even sacrificed a sheep on her father's threshold
as a guarantee of his intentions—but Driss was
proud to have written the first "modern" marriage contract in the history of Meknes. He had
paid his half of the *sdaq* on the night of the wedding, but two weeks later Fatna had failed her
stenographers' examination and was told that she
would have to spend another year in school.
Lately, Omar had been asking Dawia if she

thought they would ever see the money that was still owed them. Fatna fought with her mother-in-law all day and kept coming home to Sidi Yussef. And Driss, for his part, had been threatening to take another wife if Fatna failed her examination again. He said that he was a modern man and wanted a modern wife, like the wives in Europe, who would earn money and make him rich.

Dawia sighed again. She had heard about men who did not want to pay properly for their wives, she told Madame Hugh, but she had never expected to have one in the family.

"It is certain that Driss will divorce me," Fatna moaned. "He says that it is *I* who must apologize. He says that *I* am to ignore all the terrible things his mother says." Fatna glared at Sidi Mohammed, who had tiptoed into the room, giggling. Then she asked Madame Hugh, "In America, does a man bring his bride to his parents' house to live?"

Madame Hugh shook her head.

Fatna thought for a minute. "Driss says that it is *hshuma* for a man to abandon his parents," she said. "Driss says that even the King lives with his mother."

"But they say that the King has *three* wives," Madame Hugh said, smiling.

"And soon, Allah willing, he will have four wives," Musa added. He had heard that Hassan II was looking for a new wife—one he could take out of the country on his state visits. Hassan's first three wives were said to be in purdah in the palace and could not be seen by strangers. And when Hassan travelled, with no one along to sit to the right of his host at dinner, there were always complicated problems of protocol. As it happened, the King had just been invited to a state dinner, and Madame Hugh had said that all the diplomats in Rabat were wondering what the King was going to do. There were already rumors concerning a young lady from Casablanca. Some of the girl's paternal uncles had been made judges, and the Widow Rabha had heard talk of a royal wedding on her radio.

"It is better for the King to go away alone," Dawia announced, pulling up her own towel and draping it modestly around her.

Fatna began to cry. Musa looked at her, blushing. He stood up to go, but before he could offer the polite excuses, Driss and his mother arrived. They were preceded by a loud crashing sound and a sudden tremor in the walls of the courtyard, which signalled to the family that Driss had just driven his new Renault into the side of Dawia's house. Driss had driven into the house twice before, so no one but Madame Hugh was at all surprised.

Dawia walked calmly to the door, opened it, and waved to Driss and his mother in the automo-

bile. Driss was screaming curses at his steering
wheel. He had bought the Renault last month,
with most of his bakshish savings, but he had
never really mastered the art of driving it. The
bumper of his car was bent like a Berber pastry,
as Musa noted, and both the headlights were
smashed. When Driss climbed out to inspect the
latest damage, Dawia laughed, delighted, into
her towel. Even Fatna grinned.

"I am taking you home," Driss said to Fatna.
He pointed to his mother, Kinza, in the car. "You
see, my mother is here to tell you to come home."

Kinza, who was wrapped in a thick black jellaba and a long veil, nodded grimly through the
open window. It had been her first automobile
ride. Fatna walked over to embrace her. Dawia
followed.

"It is a great burden for us all—what Khadija
has done," Kinza told Dawia. "There has never
been such a terrible thing in our family."

"It is a terrible thing," Dawia agreed.

"I have decided that it is best to forget the
matter of the penicillin," Kinza said.

Dawia turned to tell Fatna, but the girl had
run back into the house to avoid the neighbors,
who had heard the crash and come to their doors
to listen. Driss went in after her. They stayed in
the house for a long time, shouting at each other.
When they finally came out, Fatna was carrying

her purple lipstick. Her three best caftans were folded over her arm.

"This must not happen again," Driss announced, to no one in particular. "She has already lost a half day's practice at stenographers' school."

Friday, July 7th: Dawia awoke this morning and prayed for word from Sidi Kacem. She washed her floors, scrubbed her teapots, and opened a bottle of Coca-Cola for Abderrahman, Ali, Sidi Mohammed, and Saida, but when she unwound her towel for little Jmaa, her milk was dry. She had barely eaten for days. The neighbors were saying that she was getting thin and pale, like Madame Hugh, and she knew that soon they would be saying that Omar ben Allel could not afford to feed his wife. Last night, she had even

77

refused a couscous that the Widow Rabha brought her. The seven old women from the alley, who arrived to keep their vigil soon after Fatna left for the *medina,* had eaten the couscous instead.

The seven old women were back in Dawia's courtyard today, and the Widow Rabha was with them. Abderrahman, Ali, Sidi Mohammed, and Saida, who were all afraid of the Widow Rabha, were hiding in the *bit ddyaf,* but Jmaa, who was too young to be afraid of anything, had just crawled onto her lap and was drooling hungrily on her clean jellaba.

The Widow Rabha was a small, bony woman with protruding gold teeth and a look of gloating and imperious propriety. She tracked scandal with the persistence of a hungry Sahara jackal— they liked to say in Sidi Yussef that fear of the Widow Rabha's tongue did more to encourage respectability than all the teachings of the Prophet and the saints combined—and she was never more content than when she was presiding over scandals that involved the daughters of her friends. The Widow Rabha herself was cursed with five unmarried daughters, all of them ugly and all of them unquestionably pure. (Rabha's husband had been heard to murmur on his deathbed that he was happy to escape having to feed five virgins into their old age.) Rabha was proud to say that none of her daughters had ever gone walking unescorted, and that Azziza, the eldest, mindful of the great temptation she presented to the men of the quarter, had not even ventured out of her own small corner of Sidi Yussef for the past two years. Azziza was a spinster of twenty. She had a mustache, and she weighed almost a hundred kilos, and in the memory of the neighbors no one had ever knocked on the Widow Rabha's door with a solid offer for the girl's hand. Musa often told his friends that the girl should be sent to Marrakech, where the men had stronger tastes in women, but the subject of Azziza was very delicate, and he had never spoken of this to the Widow Rabha herself.

Dawia, pouring tea for the women, listened to the Widow Rabha talk about all the invitations she had refused from her rich, widowed brother-in-law, who lived alone in the *medina* and owned a television set. The Widow Rabha was saying that in the interests of her good name she had had to forfeit the distinction of being the only woman in Sidi Yussef ever to have watched television. Dawia thought about this for a moment, and then she offered to send Abderrahman to the *medina* in the Widow Rabha's place. Abderrahman, she said, could come back and report to the Widow Rabha in detail on all the programs he had seen. Both women had heard a great deal about television. There was a joke the men in Sidi Yussef liked to tell about a country Berber who bought a television set. Each day, they said, the Berber watched his television, and it revealed to him everything of importance that was happening in the universe. One night, however, the Berber's cow died. But the Berber did not discover that his cow was dead until the following morning. Furious, he kicked in the screen of the television set and beat the box to pieces with a club. "If you know everything, you devil, why didn't you tell me that my cow was dying?" the Berber shouted. The television has not revealed anything to the Berber since then.

Dawia called Abderrahman and told him to leave at once for the *medina,* but before Abderrahman could find his slippers, Mustafa came running into the courtyard. He had just returned from Sidi Kacem, and he was grinning triumphantly. Dawia and the old women crowded around him. The Widow Rabha stayed on her mat, at a modest distance across the courtyard. The women whispered that Mustafa was looking splendid in his Gibraltar suit.

"It is exactly as I have said," Mustafa told Dawia. "Omar is very lucky to have brothers who know the *souks.* I ask you to name another man in Sidi Yussef who has two such brothers."

Dawia shook her head, unable to reply.

"We arrived in Sidi Kacem Wednesday night before eleven, thanks to our good friend Abdeslam," Mustafa began. "And we went directly to the home of our friend from the market. Our friend had seen Khadija at the house of one of his neighbors—an old woman who has many rooms and rents them to men. The men come to her with girls who are not their wives." Mustafa lowered his voice and added, "And sometimes, if the men cannot find girls who are exactly right, they give *her* money and she helps them."

All the old women began to ululate. It was the custom of Moroccan women to ululate—they called it youyouing—during wars, weddings, circumcisions, and other potentially disastrous events.

"And then we all drank tea together," Mustafa said.

Dawia started to ask about her daughter, but the old women told her not to interrupt the story.

"After we had drunk the tea, we went to the old woman's house and knocked on her door." Mustafa paused dramatically. He liked telling stories, and on Friday afternoons he often would listen to the storytellers in the public square outside the tomb of Sheikh el Kamel in order to improve his style. "We knocked from midnight until precisely three in the morning," he went on. Like Omar, he owned a wristwatch and enjoyed telling time.

The women youyoued again.

"At last, it was decided that something different should be done," Mustafa said.

"It is clear that the wicked old woman did not want to open her door!" the Widow Rabha called across the courtyard.

"Exactly," Mustafa said. "And so it was decided that Omar and our friend from Sidi Kacem would go to the Commissariat to find a policeman. At first, our friend said no—the old woman is his neighbor, and he did not want problems with her—but then I had an excellent thought." Mustafa paused again. "I told him that the police would do nothing to the old woman, since the police are also her neighbors and did not want problems with her themselves."

"Ah, that was very good," one of the old women remarked.

"It is *hshuma* to arrest your neighbor," another old woman said.

"And so Omar and our friend went with Abdeslam to the Commissariat," Mustafa continued. "Mokhtar stayed by the door, and I climbed up onto the roof to make sure that no one escaped while they were gone. It was very difficult, climbing onto the roof. It was just like a film, only more difficult."

All the women looked at Mustafa admiringly.

"And it was very dangerous, too," Mustafa said. "Later, I asked Omar, 'How many brothers would be brave enough to climb a roof like that?' "

"And then?" Dawia asked him. Saida and Sidi

Mohammed had crept into the courtyard, and they were clinging to Dawia's skirt, listening.

"At four, the men returned to the house with two policemen," Mustafa told her. "At first, the policemen had said that they would not come. They said that they were obliged to arrest criminals only during the day, between nine and twelve in the morning and three and six in the afternoon. But then Abdeslam suggested that Omar would pay twenty-five dirhams for an arrest, and they were very happy."

"He is a clever man, that Abdeslam," one of the old women cut in. The other women nodded.

"The two policemen knocked at the door," Mustafa went on. " 'Open your door!' they said. 'We are policemen.' But the old woman still would not open her door, and so the policemen took out their revolvers and shot through the lock."

Dawia began to youyou all alone.

"The old woman was screaming, and there was a man in her courtyard, standing on a suitcase, trying to escape onto the roof," Mustafa said. "The policemen seized the man. Oh, he was a terrible type. Ugly, like a demon. I asked myself, 'How could the girl have gone with such a terrible type?' "

"My Azziza would not have gone with a man like that," the Widow Rabha said.

Abderrahman stuck out his tongue at her.

Mustafa ignored them both and added, "I said to Omar, 'Look at that criminal! How many brothers would wait alone on a roof with a criminal like him around?' "

Dawia tapped Mustafa on the arm. "Khadija?" she said.

Mustafa, who did not like being interrupted in the middle of a story, stopped talking and sulked. After a long time, he said, "Of course the girl was there. Why wouldn't she be there? There was a well in the courtyard, and the man had said that he would throw her in if she ever tried to leave the house."

Dawia gasped, and murmured the names of several saints.

"The man had bought her many new clothes," Mustafa added. "Caftans and bloomers. Even a jellaba."

"Ah," the old women said, looking impressed.

"The girl was very unhappy," Mustafa told them. "No one would let her take the clothes to the Commissariat with her."

Saturday, July 8th: Today, at noon, the pilgrims on their way to the tomb of the great saint Moulay Idriss saw Monsieur Hugh's blue Opel parked off the winding mountain road that led to the entrance to the sacred city. Dawia was standing beside it, wrapped in a long, pink towel that was flapping a little in the warm breeze. Jmaa, slung in a fold of the towel, snored softly on her back as she squinted up into the sunlight, trying to get a glimpse of Moulay Idriss's tomb. No woman had been permitted to enter the tomb

85

since a drop of blood was discovered on the floor
there, many years ago, and the whole shrine had
to be purified, at great expense to the saint's
descendants, who declared it to be the blood of an
unclean female. Now, whenever Dawia visited
Moulay Idriss, she liked looking at the tomb,
which reminded her of the fine purity of Islam.
Once, a *fqih* in Sidi Yussef had told Dawia that
a woman who was unclean during a pilgrimage to
the holy city of Mecca must make the pilgrimage
again, another year. Dawia had been very much
impressed with this pious information. "Her pilgrimage counts for nothing in the eyes of Allah,"
she always said now when she repeated the story
for her friends.

Today, Dawia was on her way to the Gendarmerie Royale to claim her daughter. ("The
girl was stolen on the mountain, so naturally the
crime belongs to the Gendarmerie at Moulay
Idriss," Omar had said, with authority, when he
returned from Sidi Kacem last night and announced that Khadija and her abductor, a wandering *souk* musician by the name of Mohammed
ben Mohammed ben Mohammed, had been sent
to Moulay Idriss in a long black police van.)
Dawia had set out early in the morning with
Omar, Fatna, and Monsieur Hugh—Fatna had
just come home again, carrying her caftans and
complaining that she had been grievously insulted
at breakfast by her mother-in-law—but Fatna
kept getting carsick, and Monsieur Hugh had

86

already had to stop because of her three times. At the moment, Fatna was squatting behind a large rock, vomiting. Omar and Monsieur Hugh were pacing near the rock, trying to decide what to do with her. When Fatna stood up, she remarked bitterly that her lace veil and her new white summer jellaba were soiled. She had put them on especially for her trip to Moulay Idriss, after hearing from Musa, who had stopped by this morning on his way to the goat *souk,* that Monsieur le Chef de Gendarmerie was a handsome young bachelor looking for a wife.

"I am killing myself because of that *hisha mwusskha,*" Fatna hissed, cursing her sister. *"Hisha mwusskha"* were the words for "filthy beast," and Fatna repeated them as she ran back to the car, tripping over stones and flowers in her high heels.

The Gendarmerie Royale at Moulay Idriss was a little white building perched on a row of wooden stilts, with a guard at the door and two benches in the front hallway. When Dawia, Omar, and Monsieur Hugh arrived—they had left Fatna at the saint's spring to wash the spots off her jellaba—Mohammed ben Mohammed ben Mohammed was handcuffed to one of the benches. Khadija was waiting on the other bench. She was staring at Mohammed ben Mohammed ben Mohammed, and she did not look up to meet her mother's eyes.

Khadija was thin and drawn. There were deep-

87

purple shadows under her brown eyes, which
stared out of their bony sockets like the glass eyes
of the skeletons in an American horror movie
that Omar once had seen in the *ville nouvelle*.
Her face was smeared with dirt, her hair was
snarled, there were sores on her mouth, and
two of her big yellow front teeth were gone. Her
clothes reeked. They were the same red sweater
and black school skirt that she had worn to the
musem of Sidi Ahmed and Sidi Ali.

Dawia ran down the hallway to embrace her
daughter, and then she settled down on the floor
at Khadija's feet. Omar waited at the door,
frowning. He was holding a shabby jellaba and
a veil that was ragged and faded and full of holes.
Finally, he flung them both at Khadija. "Here.
You are a woman now—cover yourself decently,"
he said.

When Khadija had put the jellaba on and tied
the veil into place across her face, Monsieur
Hugh walked up to her and took her hand.
"Khadija?" he said softly.

Khadija kept staring at Mohammed ben Mohammed ben Mohammed and did not answer him.

"Everything will be all right," Monsieur Hugh
said.

Monsieur le Chef de Gendarmerie, who had
been out all morning looking for the caid's bicycle, walked into the hallway just as Monsieur
Hugh was speaking. Fatna was with him—they

had met outside, when Monsieur le Chef de Gendarmerie stopped to admire the Opel and found Fatna, at the car mirror, applying a gleaming coat of lipstick—and she was looking very pleased with herself. There were no spots on her new white jellaba now.

"I am happy to see that you have come to visit," Monsieur le Chef de Gendarmerie said, in French, to Monsieur Hugh. "Perhaps, one day soon, we will have the opportunity to discuss American automobiles."

Fatna stepped between them, coughing. "Ah, what a tragedy!" she cried. "What a terrible thing to bear!" She turned to Monsieur Hugh, moaning. "Feel my heart," she said. "Feel how the heart of a respectable woman is beating."

Monsieur Hugh looked alarmed and began backing away.

Fatna smiled wanly at Monsieur le Chef de Gendarmerie. "*You* may feel how my heart is beating," she told him.

Dawia hid her head in her towel.

Monsieur le Chef de Gendarmerie put his hand out tentatively. "Her heart is certainly beating," he said to Monsieur Hugh.

Monsieur Hugh shrugged.

"I am coming to Meknes next week," Monsieur le Chef de Gendarmerie continued. "Perhaps we will have the opportunity to talk about automobiles then."

"What about the girl?" Monsieur Hugh asked him.

Dawia looked up. No one had told her yet how Khadija was stolen.

"Would you prefer the girl's story or the story of Mohammed ben Mohammed ben Mohammed?" Monsieur le Chef de Gendarmerie asked them.

Monsieur Hugh said that he preferred Khadija's story. Dawia agreed.

Monsieur le Chef de Gendarmerie led everyone into his office but the guard, Khadija, and Mohammed ben Mohammed ben Mohammed. According to the girl, he began, sitting down behind his big desk, Mohammed ben Mohammed ben Mohammed had met her on the path between the tombs of Sidi Ali ben Hamdush and Sidi Ahmed Dghughi. He was carrying a beautiful guitar, and he invited her into a tent, where there were many musicians and dancing girls, to hear him play. Then he offered her a glass of tea. There must have been hashish—or some powerful magic verses—in the tea, Monsieur le Chef de Gendarmerie went on, since the next thing the girl remembered was waking up in Sidi Kacem, at the old woman's house. "And the girl is no longer a virgin," he concluded his story. "She has just been examined at the dispensary."

"What did you expect?" Monsieur Hugh asked him. "Did you expect that the girl would be a prisoner for twenty days and come home a virgin?"

"Who can predict the will of Allah?" Monsieur le Chef de Gendarmerie said grandly. Then he stood up, clicked his heels, bowed to Monsieur Hugh, and excused himself. He had a new report on the caid's bicycle to write.

"Hisha mwusskha! Hisha mwusskha!" Fatna snapped at her sister as soon as everyone had left the office.

"Look at him," Omar said, pointing a finger at Mohammed ben Mohammed ben Mohammed. "He is horrible, horrible."

"What's the matter with *you?*" Monsieur Hugh asked Omar.

"How could she go with such a horrible man?" Omar said.

"You wanted her back, and now you blame her," Monsieur Hugh told him. "You act as if it were *her* fault."

"She has disgraced her father," Omar said stubbornly.

"Hisha mwusskha!" Fatna said.

Dawia slipped a fresh fig out of a fold in her towel and began to eat again.

Sunday, July 9th: Everyone in Sidi Yussef wanted to look at Khadija today. The seven old women came youyouing back to Dawia's courtyard. The neighbors came, and brought their children. And even Zahara, with Bushta's kind permission, came visiting. Dawia spent the whole morning making tea for her company, and at noon she was still at the brazier in her little kitchen, waiting for a fresh kettle of water to boil. She was always very careful in making tea. Once, when she was a bride of nearly twelve and living

93

in the country, she had let the water in her kettle boil over into a brazier, and Aisha Qandisha, who lived in all fires, had attacked her for the first time. Dawia had fallen to the floor, paralyzed and crying with pain, and for three days and three nights the finest musician in her village had had to sit by her side with his reed flute, searching for the *rih* that would make her dance and drive the devil away. Later, when she was cured, Omar had gone to the *souk* and bought a young black goat to sacrifice over the brazier, on the very spot where Dawia had been struck. Dawia drank the goat's blood. Since then, she watched her kettle conscientiously to see that not a drop of water ever spilled.

While Dawia waited in the kitchen, she chatted with the Widow Rabha about her guests. She would have liked to have a room for the women, she said, but Fatna had shut herself up in the red room and was refusing to unlock the door. Dawia had heard Fatna, through the wall, practicing what she would say to her husband and his mother when they came to get her, and she told Rabha that the girl had decided to ask them for a new lipstick and a European pocketbook. Earlier this morning, she said, she had had to stop Omar from breaking down the door and beating Fatna with his stick. It was always unwise to beat a married daughter; Dawia knew of a case in Sidi Yussef in which the husband had brought his father-in-law to court and sued for damages to private property. She had decided, therefore, to leave the room to Fatna, the courtyard to the women and children, and the *bit dyaf* to Omar and the men. The *bit dyaf* always belonged to the man of the family. All his wealth was on display there—his pillows, his carpets, and his silver-plated teapot— for his friends to appreciate or, if no friends happened to be visiting, for the man to appreciate by himself. Last night, Omar had gone into the *bit dyaf* and sat for many hours, contemplating his pillows, which were blue with white pineapples, and mumbling curses at Monsieur Hugh, who had made him swear in the name of Allah to stay calm. Dawia had left him alone there, and she had tried her best to keep the children away. She knew that in the big houses of the *medina* women and children were never permitted in the *bit dyaf*. But, as she remarked to the Widow Rabha, in Sidi Yussef there was rarely enough space in a house for such good form.

Dawia poured the water from her kettle into a teapot nearly full of sugar and mint leaves, and then she carried it into the courtyard, where Khadija was sitting on a mat with Zahara and the women and children. Jmaa was sleeping on Khadija's lap, and Saida and Sidi Mohammed were snuggled up beside her, smiling. Earlier, Dawia had said that the devil left Khadija as soon as the girl was with her little brothers and sisters. By now, Khadija was sad only when her father hurried by her with his head turned. Omar had not spoken to Khadija all day.

"You cannot imagine how my family missed me," Khadija was saying to the women when Dawia squatted on the mat to pour the tea. "Everyone was sick while I was away."

"It is a terrible thing for a family," the Widow Rabha remarked, joining them.

"My father, especially—he was very sick," Khadija went on. "Every day, he went to Fatna's husband for a penicillin shot."

"Ah, he must have been very, very sick," one of the old women said. She had heard that Driss's injections were not cheap.

"And my mother," Khadija said, turning to Dawia. "My mother was sick, too. She fell down all the time."

Dawia looked pleased. "Yes," she said. "I was very sick. I was even sicker than Omar. I could not sleep. I could not eat—"

"But it was not my fault," Khadija cut in. "Yesterday, Monsieur Hugh said to my father, 'Remember, she is only a child and it is not her fault.' "

"That is true," Dawia remarked. "That is exactly what he said."

"And my teacher said so, too," Khadija said. Her teacher was a Toulousain, on loan from the French government. He had come to Sidi Yussef late in June, to ask why Khadija was not in school for her examinations, and again yesterday, after Madame Hugh had called to tell him that the girl was home.

"He wants me to come back to school in September," Khadija said proudly. "He said that being absent from school because you are stolen is not the same as being absent because you are a bad girl. He said that everybody would forgive me."

"Well, perhaps," the Widow Rabha said.

The old women shook their heads.

"But I am not going back to school," Khadija went on, looking down sadly at her scrawny arms and legs. "I am too thin."

"It is true, she cannot go back to school," Dawia said. "No one will forget. They will all talk about her."

"And the men will follow her," the Widow Rabha added. "It is always that way when a girl has lost her reputation."

"And everyone will laugh at me," Khadija said, handing Jmaa to her mother.

"Then you will have to marry an ugly old man like Bushta," Zahara announced, giggling. She was a husky, cheerful girl with bright-red cheeks, and she was admired by all the women in the family but Fatna because of her hairy legs. Hairy legs were considered a sign of great fertility.

Khadija made a face at her aunt and giggled, too.

"So what I have heard is true," the Widow

Rabha said to Zahara. "Your future husband is old and ugly."

"He is *horrible*," Zahara agreed. "I love the melon merchant, but my brothers have decided, and there is nothing I can do. They will not sign the marriage act with anyone but Bushta."

All the women chuckled sympathetically. As far as any of them knew, no Moroccan woman had ever managed to get married without the permission of her nearest male relative. It was her father or her brother who accepted the proposal, conducted the bargaining, and concluded the negotiations as her "matrimonial representative," and the virgin was said to have given her hearty consent to the arrangements if she laughed, cried, sighed, or simply blushed and was silent before the marriage judge. According to holy Malikite law, the right to be represented in a marriage by her father or her brother was "a right in the favor of the woman," since it protected her, in her innocence, from unscrupulous types who might steal her inheritance or refuse to pay her bride price. Thinking about their rights always amused the women of Sidi Yussef.

"It is because Bushta is rich that my uncles want him for Zahara," Khadija told them.

"He is rich, but he is hideous," Zahara said cheerfully.

"He *is hideous*," Khadija said.

Zahara burst out laughing, and for a minute

the two girls rolled across the floor, whooping at each other. Then, suddenly, Khadija pushed her aunt away, sat up straight, and stared at the old women. "The man said that he would throw me in the well," she said. "He said that I would never see my family again. My father was sick the whole time that I was gone."

Monday, July 10th: The Tribunal of the Province of Meknes met in the *ville nouvelle* in the Palais de Justice, a massive concrete building that was just down the street from the post office and that had a large mural in its lobby of Arabs and Berbers working happily together for a modern Morocco. Both the mural and the Palais de Justice itself were the inspiration of Frenchmen. During their protectorate, the Frenchmen had wanted a monument worthy of the Code Napoléon, which they were importing, clause by clause, along with

101

pigs, cheese, wine, and some of their other favorite institutions, and it was said by the native Meknasiyyin that the Palais they built was as long and as difficult to find your way around in as the Code itself. In the old religious court in the *medina,* the judges, in their red fezzes, sat in shady little rooms off lovely courtyards, contemplating the flowers and the fountains as they dictated marriage acts, divorces, and inheritance settlements according to ancient Malikite law and to the amounts of bakshish involved. But in the Palais de Justice there were judges with ermine trimming on their jellabas. *They* had French technical assistants, and dealt out an odd new justice in gloomy gray courtrooms with fluorescent lights. Musa, who liked going to the Palais every now and then to amuse himself, once said that only the bakshish changing hands was the same in the old courts and the new ones.

It was nine in the morning when Dawia, Omar, and Musa brought Khadija to the Palais de Justice to see the *juge d'instruction,* who was going to decide what crimes had been committed by Mohammed ben Mohammed ben Mohammed and whether a case could be presented at the first fall session of the criminal court. Dawia and Khadija immediately settled into opposite corners of a long bench in a narrow corridor and began peering fearfully at a door that was marked "M. le Juge d'Instruction." Omar paced the corridor

with Musa, smiling to himself. He said that by
fall, after a hot summer in prison in preventive
detention, Mohammed ben Mohammed ben Mohammed should be willing to pay a handsome
compensation for Khadija's lost bride price, in
the hope of arranging for a short sentence. According to a report that the public prosecutor had
left on the judge's desk this morning, Mohammed
ben Mohammed ben Mohammed had violated
Articles 486, 471, and 436, respectively, of the
new Moroccan penal code when he so unwisely
raped, kidnapped, and sequestered Khadija, and
could be kept in prison forty years for all his
crimes. He had also apparently drugged a minor,
but inasmuch as the prosecutor had mislaid his
mimeographed translation of the drug laws—and
since his French technical assistant, who could
have read him the originals, was at the beach in
Casablanca on vacation—the prosecutor had decided that for the time being it was best to overlook the question of drugs.

The corridor of the Palais was crowded this
morning, and Dawia and Khadija kept their veils
well up over their noses, and their hands—
Khadija had hennaed her fingernails for the occasion—clasped modestly. A group of peasants
waiting to see the judge about a mule thief in
their village had just sat down by Dawia. And
down the bench toward Khadija there were two
prostitutes from the brothel quarter of the city

who had neglected to pay the police their yearly
bakshish; a fierce-looking Berber from the mountains who had been apprehended last night in the
medina chasing Arabs with a blunderbuss; and a
shy lady poisoner from a nearby *bidonville*.
Twelve prisoners, handcuffed in pairs, squatted
in a row farther down the corridor. And behind
them, on an otherwise empty bench, Mohammed
ben Mohammed ben Mohammed and a young
sergeant from the Gendarmerie sat handcuffed
together. Mohammed was indeed ugly. His eyes
were bleary; his mustache drooped, untrimmed;
his face was gray with stubble; and he had on the
same baggy blue trousers and white beanie that
he had been wearing Wednesday night in Sidi
Kacem. He was chewing nervously at the fingernails on his free hand, and he did not look up
when the sergeant called Omar over and handed
him a copy of Khadija's medical report, which
Omar would need for his meeting with the *juge
d'instruction*. The sergeant wanted fifty-five dirhams for the report.

Omar borrowed the fifty-five dirhams from
Musa and got the report—it was signed and
stamped, and it stated categorically that Khadija
was no longer negotiable as a virgin—and then
he and Musa squeezed onto the bench between
Dawia and the peasants.

Dawia was yawning. She had been up all night,
listening to Omar rehearse a story that he felt

would please the *juge d'instruction*. Omar had decided to say that Mohammed ben Mohammed ben Mohammed had approached his daughter in Sidi Ahmed's tomb, where she was praying devoutly, and told her that he had been sent there to escort her safely down the footpath to her father's tent. When Omar had perfected his story, he woke Khadija and repeated it to her. This morning, however, he happened to mention to Khadija that he intended never to let her out of the house again, and Khadija, who liked taking walks and going swimming with her friends in the public pool in the *medina*, was still furious at him. Dawia did not know now whether Khadija would tell the proper story to the *juge d'instruction*.

"You must tell her not to mention Abdeslam," Dawia whispered to Omar. She said that any talk of a trip to El Hajeb with Abdeslam would lose them the price of a good *sdaq* from Mohammed ben Mohammed ben Mohammed's relatives.

Omar called down the bench to his daughter, but by the time Khadija had made her way past the Berber, the whores, the lady poisoner, and the peasants and was sitting beside him, the janitor in charge of the corridor was standing over Omar with his mop and pail, waiting to hear what Omar had to say. There was a knife tattooed on the janitor's forearm, which meant that once he had gone to prison for a violent crime. Musa had often talked about the Palais de Justice janitors

and their knife tattoos. Now he whispered to
Dawia that the janitors had bought their freedom
with the gossip they collected cleaning corridors.
Dawia agreed with him. She, too, had been to the
Palais de Justice before. In 1958, at her mother's
suggestion, she had come to complain about
Omar, who had beaten her up with his stick for
giving away bread to neighbors. Omar, however,
had arrived in court carrying a new blue caftan,
and they had settled their argument.

"It is necessary to tell the truth," Omar announced, grinning sheepishly up at the janitor.

"The truth is the important thing," Dawia
said.

The janitor wandered away, muttering.

"If I tell the truth, can I go to the swimming
pool this afternoon?" Khadija asked her father.

Omar shook his head.

"But I will be much more careful this time,"
Khadija insisted.

"What is the use of having daughters?" Omar
said.

Musa, who was getting very sensitive on the
subject of daughters, tapped Omar on the arm.
"Perhaps, to pass the time, I will finish my
story," he suggested. He had been reciting his
favorite *Paris-Match* prisoner-of-war story for
Omar, and by now, after several sessions at the
Sidi Yussef coffeehouse, he had got his hero—an
American flier, shot down over North Vietnam—

out of his burning airplane and into a clearing
in the woods, where he was surrounded by
enemy. At the mention of a story, the peasants
next to Musa and Omar looked up, and the
prisoners on the floor leaned forward attentively.

"The American is very, very tired," Musa began. "He has been walking and hiding in the
woods for three days, and so, although the enemy
is everywhere, he decides that he will sleep for a
few minutes and refresh himself."

"Who is the enemy?" one of the prisoners
asked him.

"The enemy is the enemy of the American,"
Musa said. "The story does not specify."

"Perhaps it is the Jews," Dawia said. She had
heard from Driss that the Jews were everybody's
enemy. And last week, in a dream, Aisha Qandisha had told her that the Jews ate pig and were
not circumcised.

"It is possible," Musa said politely. "But I do
not think so. Now, then, when the American
wakes up, he sees that it is morning and that he
has slept for many hours, and he says to himself,
'*Oh là là,* I have lost time. If I do not hurry, the
enemy will find me.'"

"Perhaps it would be best to see the lawyer
after all," Omar cut in. He was referring to a
Meknasi Jew by the name of Solomon, whom the
anciens combattants in Sidi Yussef had hired
many years ago to take a case against one of the

107

Pasha's deputies to court. When the deputy lost his job and all his power, the *anciens combattants* agreed that there had been some very powerful Jewish devils on Maître Solomon's side. Omar, for one, had never forgotten the lawyer, and lately he had been saying that with Maître Solomon and his Jewish devils representing him he would be certain to get a good *sdaq* in damages. When Omar was a boy, there were tribal Jews all over Morocco, but now only a few thousand city Jews remained. These Jews were rich and clever, and the King protected them. Driss wanted to kill them, as the Egyptians were doing, or put them in camps in the Sahara, as the Algerians had done, but Omar always told him that the Jews made good lawyers and even better magicians, and that it was much more practical to leave them alone.

"To hire Solomon—that would be a good joke on Mohammed ben Mohammed ben Mohammed," Omar said, chuckling.

Several of the prisoners gestured impatiently, and one of them called to Musa to get on with his story.

"Just then," Musa said, clearing his throat, "just then the American sees some men creeping into the clearing. They are wearing uniforms that are just like the American's uniform, and he believes that they are his friends—"

"Praise be to Allah!" one of the peasants interrupted.

"But they are not his friends," Musa said. "They are the enemy, and they run after the American and seize him, and the one among them who is their chief tells them to tie up the American and beat him with their rifles. Then the American faints." Musa paused dramatically, and went on, "As soon as the American wakes up, they take him to an ant hole under a tree and push his face into it. The ants are very dangerous. They enter the American's nostrils and his ears, and they bite the poor American until his face is swollen and sore. Then the enemy marches with him to a place where there is a deep hole, like a well, and they put the American in the hole and close it with a big stone."

"Look, they are taking Mohammed ben Mohammed ben Mohammed to the judge!" Dawia said suddenly. She pointed to the sergeant from Moulay Idriss, who had unlocked Mohammed's handcuffs and was pulling him toward the judge's door. All the other prisoners stared at Mohammed.

"It's not so bad in prison!" one of the prisoners called out. "Wait and see—you'll be fat like us soon!"

The prisoners, who were all very scrawny, laughed and rattled their handcuffs. Their guard —an old policeman from the Commissariat— shouted at them to stop, and the janitor, running down the corridor, hurled his scrub brush at the prisoner who had talked. One of the whores on the bench jumped up and kissed the prisoner's head.

Musa, who was eager to continue his story, coughed pointedly. "The poor American spends the whole night in the well," he said. "And then, in the morning, the enemy takes him out, and they all walk until they come to a village where there are many huts. They put heavy chains on the American's legs and throw him into one of these huts and lock the door. It is very dark in the hut, and much time passes before the American can see the men who are in there with him. They are all prisoners, and they are all very thin. That is to say, nearly dead. The American asks them, 'How long have you been in this terrible place, my friends?' One of the prisoners says, 'Me? One month.' Another prisoner, who is about to die, says, 'Three months.'"

Just then, Mohammed ben Mohammed ben Mohammed walked out of the judge's office. The sergeant from the Gendarmerie, who had been waiting by the door, snapped his dangling handcuff back onto Mohammed and hustled him along the corridor. They disappeared down a flight of stairs that led to an interrogation room.

"They are going to beat Mohammed," Musa whispered to Omar and Dawia.

Omar smiled. "Ah, that is very good for us," he said.

"Now I will tell you how the Americans in the

hut are fed," Musa said, nodding graciously to the peasants and the prisoners, and to the Berber, the whores, the lady poisoner, and the Commissariat policeman, who were also listening. "The enemy soldiers hunt in the morning for rabbits. They eat their part, and then they leave the rest in the sun until it is spoiled and give it to the poor prisoners."

"Oh, that is not kind," Dawia said.

"And when there are no rabbits to be found, the enemy is very angry and fires on the prisoners' hut and kills many prisoners that way," Musa went on. "One day, a frog enters the hut, and the prisoners kill it and divide the meat. The American gets the heart of the frog for his part. He says to his friends, 'The heart of a frog is nothing in the eyes of Allah, but it is a meal just the same.'"

The two whores were called to see the *juge d'instruction,* and then the peasants were called. The peasants were reluctant to leave the corridor with the fate of the American unresolved. One of them, a stocky little man in an old work shirt and baggy black overalls, looked frightened as he padded, barefoot, toward the judge's door. He was shuddering badly when he and the others came out. Suddenly, with a jerk, he stiffened. Then he fell. His face turned red, and strange gurgling noises rose in his throat. In seconds, he was in convulsions. Urine was seeping down the legs of his overalls, and foam began to spill out of the corners of his mouth. One of the peasant women threw herself on top of him to hold him down.

"You see, here is someone who has been struck by the devil," Dawia told her daughter.

Khadija giggled and turned away.

"Monsieur Hugh says that it is not the devil," Musa told them. "He says that it is a *nesrani* sickness called epilepsy."

Dawia thought for a minute. "No, it is the devil," she said.

"Of course it is the devil," Omar said. He was fumbling in his pocket for a jackknife that he always carried, and as soon as he found it he ran to the peasant and began stabbing at the floor around the peasant's head.

Dawia told Musa that Omar was driving the peasant's devil away.

"Get him up! Get him up!" the janitor shouted, rushing up and poking at the peasant with a long broom. Omar and the woman ignored him. The janitor cursed them. He threw down his broom, grabbed the peasant's legs, and started to drag the peasant to the end of the corridor. Omar crawled after them, stabbing the floor. Little by little, the peasant's convulsions subsided. The strange noises in his throat gave way to short, gagging coughs. Then he slept.

"There is filth all over my floor," the janitor

screamed down the corridor. "What will it be the next time?"

Nobody listened to him. The other peasants, the prisoners, the Berber, the whores, the lady poisoner, and the policeman were all busy talking about Musa's story.

"You are making too much noise!" the janitor shouted. "From now on, you are permitted to talk only to the person next to you!"

"You see, Omar has chased away the devil," Dawia said, pointing to her husband, who was sitting on the floor beside the peasant and stroking the peasant's head.

"Silence!" the janitor screamed. He hoisted the peasant by the armpits, dragged him back down the corridor, and deposited him in a heap at Dawia's feet.

Mohammed ben Mohammed ben Mohammed, on his way back from the interrogation room, tripped over the peasant. He stared for a minute, shrugged, and then sat down, at a distance, on the floor. He was drenched with sweat, and his eyes were glassy. Musa and Omar, looking at him, seemed pleased.

"And now I will continue," Musa said when he had the attention of his audience again. "One day, after many weeks in the hut, the American and three of the other prisoners decide that they are going to escape from the enemy. They wait until the enemy soldiers put down their guns to eat. Then, quickly, the prisoners creep out of their hut and seize the guns and kill everybody."

"Ah," the prisoners said. "That is very clever of them."

"And then the prisoners throw off their chains and run away," Musa went on. "They run and run, up and down the mountains, but soon two of the prisoners are very tired and they say, 'It is foolish to go by the mountains. We will separate and go by the plains.' And so they go by the plains, and the enemy sees them and kills them."

"But *that* was not very clever, going by the plains," one of the peasants said, shaking his head.

"But our friend," Musa added, "our friend and the other prisoner continue in safety over the mountains."

"Allah was with them," the lady poisoner remarked.

"But they are terribly hungry," Musa said. "And soon they have to abandon the mountains to search for food. In a forest near a river, they meet a man and ask him politely for a meal, but when the man hears that they are Americans, he takes out his axe and kills our friend's companion. Our friend saves himself in the forest, but he is all alone now, and his feet are hurting him."

The American was crawling on his belly through the enemy's rice paddies by the time Khadija and Mohammed ben Mohammed ben

Mohammed were called together to see the *juge
d'instruction*. Khadija was crying when they
came out of his office, a quarter of an hour later,
and Omar, who had been pacing again, smoking
Musa's cigarettes, stared at her so intently that
he bumped into Mohammed ben Mohammed ben
Mohammed in the middle of the corridor. Mohammed was going back to prison. He walked
away slowly, handcuffed to the sergeant, without
looking at anyone.

"He wanted to hit me," Khadija sobbed to her
mother.

"Who did?" Musa asked her. He had taken a
nap to while away the interruption, and had just
awakened.

"The judge," Khadija said. "He was very
angry, and he said that he wanted to hit me. He
even picked up his ashtray and started to throw
it, but I ducked."

"Why would he do such a thing?" Omar demanded, walking over.

"He said that I was lying," Khadija told him.
"He asked me what had happened, and then
when I told him he shouted at me. He said,
'Why are you lying to me? Why are you telling
jokes?'"

"What will become of us?" Dawia said, sighing, but before she could ask what else the judge
had told her daughter, Khadija was called back
into the judge's chamber. Omar went with her.

"Well, are we ever going to hear the end of the story?" one of the peasants asked Musa as soon as the door to the judge's office closed.

"In the name of Allah, finish your story," the prisoners on the floor grumbled. This was their third day in the corridor, and they were still waiting to see the judge.

Musa conferred with Dawia on the advisability of finishing his story in Omar's absence, and they decided that he should finish it now and repeat the ending for Omar after dinner tonight.

"The American crawls through the paddies at night, searching for food and hiding from the enemy," Musa said. "He crawls and crawls, and finally he rolls over on his back and faints. When he wakes up, it is morning, and there is a huge mountain in front of him. He thinks that he is going to die, but he knows that just beyond the mountain there are Americans, and he says to himself, 'Good. If Allah is with me, I will just have time to climb to the top of the mountain and see a small corner of liberty before dying.' Suddenly, while he is talking to himself and weeping with joy to think that he will die with a corner of liberty before his eyes, a big airplane sweeps over the valley. The American tears off his shirt to signal to the airplane, but it makes a turn and disappears over the mountain."

"Ah, the poor American!" the Berber said.

"The poor, poor American!" said the prisoners,

but then they were distracted by the sick peasant on the floor in front of them. The peasant was gagging again and trembling. The prisoners watched for a minute as his spasms quickened and the white spittle began to run from the corners of his mouth. Then they turned back to Musa.

"All is not lost," Musa continued. "Allah has not forsaken the American. The airplane sweeps down over the valley again, and the American knows for sure that his friends have seen him. He sits down on the ground to wait. Much time passes, and he is beginning to be discouraged. He thinks, Perhaps they have not seen me after all. But just then he hears the sound of a helicopter descending. There is a strange, wonderful smell coming from the helicopter, and it fills his nostrils. For a moment, he cannot remember what it is. Then, suddenly, he says to himself, 'Praise be to Allah, I am rescued! That is the strange, wonderful smell of American gasoline.'"

"Praise be to Allah!" Dawia said.

"Praise be to Allah!" said the prisoners, the peasants, the Berber, the whores, the lady poisoner, and the policeman.

Musa sat back, smiling.

Dawia, who was frightened both by the peasant's devil and by the American's enemy, covered her eyes with her hands and waited for Omar. He came out of the judge's office in a few minutes. Khadija trailed after him, in tears, but Omar was frowning and would not look back at her. He had told the judge that Khadija was carried off to Sidi Kacem on a black motorcycle, but Khadija, it appeared, had already said that she had gone to Sidi Kacem in a green bus. Dawia, hearing this, stood up to soothe her husband. The prisoners were shuffling past her now, on their way back to prison—it was nearly noon, and they would not be able to see the judge today—and the janitor was back with his broom, jabbing at the peasant at Dawia's feet and screaming "Pig!"

"It is settled—we are going to see the Jew," Omar said at last. Mohammed ben Mohammed ben Mohammed not only had told the judge that Khadija was a woman when he stole her but had also announced that his relatives in Sidi Kacem were going to hire a lawyer for him.

"I ask myself, What good does a beating do if the man remains so stubborn?" Musa remarked. "Now you will have to pay for a lawyer, too."

"The judge said, 'Why pay for a lawyer?'" Omar went on. "He told me, 'Mohammed is poor. You will not get much of a settlement from such a poor type. Why not give the girl to him immediately, and all the problems will be solved?'"

"That is very old-fashioned," Musa said.

"That is exactly what I said," Omar told him. "I said that I would never give my daughter in marriage to a man who stole her. A man like that, I said, will ask for the girl to avoid prison—and

118

to avoid paying a fair *sdaq* to her father. Then
he will divorce her." Omar stopped talking and
grinned. "And *then* I said to the judge, 'Tell me,
if Mohammed ben Mohammed ben Mohammed
is so poor, how does it happen that he has money
for a lawyer?' "

"Ah, that was very good," Musa said. "What
did the judge say to *that?*"

"The judge said, 'Good. If that is what you
want, we will arrange something between us, and
I will send the case to the Tribunal,' " Omar said.

Dawia nodded solemnly. Then she whispered
to Musa that, even now, many, many troubling
thoughts were in her head. "What happened to
the poor American?" she asked him.

"The American went to the city of New York
to eat," Musa said. "He weighed seventy-eight
kilos when the enemy seized him, but when his
friends in the helicopter found him he weighed
only thirty-eight kilos, and he was very hungry."

Tuesday, July 11th: Dawia was in her courtyard today, sifting farina onto a clay platter, when she noticed a tall man standing in the doorway, waiting for permission to enter the house. The man was beautiful, like the king of the devils, who often visited Dawia in her dreams with gifts and compliments. He was so beautiful, in fact, that Dawia stared, admiring him, for several minutes before she saw that he was only the driver Abdeslam ben Ali, and invited him in.

Abdeslam had scrubbed off all the axle grease

121

and *souk* dust that usually coated his face and hands. Today, he smelled of soap and perfumed oils and the *hammam,* rather than of mules and gasoline. In place of the rough blue overalls that he had been wearing, day and night, for more than a year now, he had put on a clean white turban and a jellaba of soft, pale linen, just like the turban and jellaba a rich Meknasi gentleman would wear to Friday mosque. And behind him, spread out across the alley for all the neighbors to see, were the hindquarters of a young sheep, still pungent and bloody from the slaughter block; three straw sacks full of eggplants and tomatoes; a golden brocade caftan; two pairs of gauzy pink bloomers; and a pair of white plastic high-heeled shoes.

Abdeslam solemnly handed the sheep and the vegetable sacks to Dawia. Then he scooped up the shoes, the caftan, and the bloomers and started walking across the courtyard to the *bit dyaf.*

"I have come to see Omar on important business," he said, knocking.

Omar opened the door to the *bit dyaf* and let him in.

Dawia dragged the sheep to a corner of the courtyard. She did not call to Khadija, who was in the kitchen, to prepare some tea for their company. Instead, she tiptoed to a small grilled window that let light and air from the courtyard into the *bit dyaf,* and squatted on the floor beside it, listening. Abdeslam spoke first. Dawia heard him ask if Omar had happened to mention to the *juge d'instruction* that unhappy incident concerning Khadija and their drive together to El Hajeb.

Half an hour later, Omar opened the door of the *bit dyaf* and beckoned to Dawia at the window, where, it appeared, he had expected to find her.

"Now make tea," Omar said, smiling. "I have found a husband for Khadija."

PART
THREE

KHADIJA

Thursday, July 20th: Khadija spent this morning posed on a carpet in the *bit dyaf.* She was waiting for Madame Hugh, who had promised to guard her while the family went to a circumcision breakfast down the alley, and she was reluctant to budge before the American had a chance to admire the golden caftan she was wearing in all its starchy and unwrinkled glory. Her father, true to his word and in spite of Abdeslam's proposal, had not let Khadija out of the house since their visit to the Palais de Justice eleven days ago. No

127

one but Musa and the seven old women who came
to visit had been able to see Khadija in her beautiful new clothes. She had been hoping to wear
her new white shoes today, along with the caftan
and a pair of the pink bloomers, but Fatna, who
for the moment was back in the *medina* with her
husband, had stolen them.

Madame Hugh arrived at ten. Khadija listened to her, in the courtyard, repeating Omar's
instructions to bolt the door and not let anybody
in while he was gone. Then she tucked her bare
feet under a pillow and carefully spread the hem
of her caftan over them.

"Well, now, so you're going to be married,"
Madame Hugh said, walking into the *bit dyaf*.

Khadija blushed and turned away.

"Are you happy, getting married?" Madame
Hugh asked her. She had collapsed onto the carpet, and she was mopping her forehead with a
handkerchief. The *smaym,* which were the forty
days of heat that Allah sent to Meknes from the
Sahara every summer, bothered Madame Hugh.
She was always sweating when she came to Sidi
Yussef. "Wouldn't you rather go to school?" she
said.

Khadija thought for a moment. "Do you like
my caftan?" she said.

"It is very beautiful," said Madame Hugh,
who was wearing blue jeans.

"And my earrings?" Khadija went on. A pair
of bright-orange plastic earrings were drooping

from her earlobes. They were her latest present from her fiancé.

"They are very beautiful, too," Madame Hugh said.

"No one in school has a caftan like mine," Khadija told her, giggling. "My husband—"

"Your *husband?*" Madame Hugh said.

"Abdeslam, who will *be* my husband," Khadija said. "He comes here every day with meat and vegetables. Two kilos of meat a day. And jewelry. And clothes. He even gives me money." Khadija, forgetting her bare feet and her crisp caftan, rolled over onto her stomach and whispered, "Yesterday, he gave me fifty dirhams."

Madame Hugh gulped. "He must love you very much," Madame Hugh said.

"Oh, he does," Khadija said. "He is going to divorce *both* his wives when we get married." She reconsidered for a moment. "The one in Meknes, anyway," she said.

"That will be nice," Madame Hugh said.

"And he is clever—much more clever than the one in prison," Khadija said. "He told my father that he was not going to pay my bride price. He said that it was up to the man who stole me to pay. Now, that was *very* clever."

"Very clever," Madame Hugh said.

"And then he said that we must not have the wedding until after the man had paid and the trial was over," Khadija went on.

"That was very clever, too," Madame Hugh

129

said. She was tugging at the zipper on a big brown pocketbook that looked to Khadija like the *shuwwaf*'s money pouch. When it was open, Madame Hugh reached inside for a pack of cigarettes.

"I want a cigarette," Khadija announced.

Madame Hugh looked surprised. She said that she had never heard of an Arab woman smoking cigarettes. It was considered *hshuma.*

"I want one," Khadija said.

"No," Madame Hugh told her. "You are too young."

"I am not too young," Khadija said. "I have been stolen, haven't I?"

Madame Hugh handed the cigarette to Khadija and lit it for her without another word.

Khadija settled back on the carpet, grinning. For a while, she lay there, puffing competently and watching the smoke she made curl up to the ceiling and dissolve in the *bit dyaf*'s dim light. "Abdeslam always gave me cigarettes," she said after a long time. "I told the judge that the man who stole me was the first one to give me cigarettes, but I only said that. It was Abdeslam."

Madame Hugh nodded.

"He would meet me on the road to school—just where the road bends—and we would drive all the way to the country," Khadija whispered confidentially. "Sometimes we would stay in the truck *all* day. He would give me money and cigarettes and candy. Chocolate candy, which is very expensive. And he would say 'I love you' all the time. He would tell me, 'I love you more than my two wives put together, and I will give you money, but you must promise me not to tell your father.' "

"My God!" Madame Hugh said.

Khadija could see that Madame Hugh was impressed. "And it wasn't even his own money," she said proudly. "It was money that belonged to Bushta. He is so stupid, that Bushta. He doesn't even know that Zahara is going to leave him after they are married. Her brothers have given her permission. They say that then she can make as much trouble as she wants, so that Bushta will divorce her. They say that they will help her, but that first she must steal all of Bushta's money for them." Khadija looked at Madame Hugh and started giggling again. "And she has already started," Khadija went on. "Every day, she asks for gifts. When Bushta comes with a caftan, she says, 'This one is not exactly right.' Or she says, 'Something has happened to this one, it is soiled.' And so Bushta buys her another caftan, and she is getting two of everything that way. My uncles are very happy. They say that once she is married she is to begin hiding things. She will say, 'I need money for the farina,' and then, when Bushta gives her the money, she will use half of it for the farina and hide the rest. Then she will say, 'Ah,

look at this, Bushta. All the farina is gone.' And
Bushta will have to give her money again." Khadija paused for a minute to smoke, and then she
said, "When Zahara was promised to Bushta, she
tried to kill herself. She sent me to the melon
merchant with a message. She said to tell him,
'My brothers will never accept you, because you
are poor and someone very rich has asked for me.'
Then she tied a cord around her neck. She was
almost dead. Her eyes were bulging and her face
was gray, like my mother's jellaba. But then her
brothers found her, and they untied the cord and
beat her and said, 'We have not fed you for sixteen years in order to lose your bride price *now*.
You are not permitted to kill yourself. You are
going to marry Bushta.' So there was nothing
to do."

"But this is awful," Madame Hugh said.

Khadija rolled over again and hugged her
friend. She told her that she had never had such a
long conversation with a *nesraniyya* before. "And
now that Abdeslam has asked for *me,* they are
worried about the money again," she went on,
delighted. "Before he asked for me, he was always visiting them with gifts and money, because
they were going to be in Bushta's family and he
did not want them to talk against him. But now
he comes to *my* father every night with gifts, instead of to their house. And so they are very worried. They have even told their mother to make
magic against me to stop the marriage."

Madame Hugh shook her head. "This is all very confusing," she said.

"Even Bushta is angry that Abdeslam has asked for me," Khadija said. "He has told my father that I am never to enter his house when he and Zahara are married, because I am a bad girl and carry messages and make problems for everyone. He was hoping that the judge would give me to Mohammed ben Mohammed ben Mohammed, and that I would live in Sidi Kacem and be too far away to carry messages." Khadija sat up suddenly. "Is it true that in America there are no virgins?" she asked her friend. Fatna has heard at the movies that it is true."

"That's what they say," Madame Hugh said, smiling.

"Then I am very modern, like an American," Khadija said, and, looking proud, she took another cigarette and slipped it under the carpet, where she was certain it would not be found.

PART
FOUR

THE WEDDING

Sunday, July 30th: Early this morning, an old woman came from the *medina* out to Sidi Yussef. She came on foot, and by the time she reached the door of a small hut in one of the back alleys, her shawls were full of dust and her throat was parched from the dry heat of the *smaym* sun. Zahara, who was spreading the morning wash on the roof of her brothers' hut, next door, saw the old woman knocking, and she called down to point her to a water pump at the end of the road.

"Hey, old woman!" Zahara shouted. "No one

is home there! They are all on a pilgrimage to Sidi Ali!"

"Tell me, is there usually a virgin in that house?" the old woman called back, taking down her veil. She was a dark, tiny thing, and her face was webbed with wrinkles and the blue crisscross tattoos of northern country women.

Zahara nodded.

"I had heard there was a virgin in the family," the old woman said. "My son is looking for a wife, and I have walked all the way from the *medina* with an offer for her father." She shrugged and added, "So I have made the trip for nothing. No one is even home to give me tea."

"Don't be depressed, old woman!" Zahara called down. "There is a young girl in *my* family! A very good young girl!"

The old woman looked up.

"Why waste your day?" Zahara said. "Why not take *her* instead?"

"That is true—why should I make the trip for nothing?" the old woman said after she had thought for a moment. "We will go together to the girl's father."

Zahara shook her head, laughing. "I am not permitted to leave my house," she told the old woman. "Go without me. Follow the alley to the pump. Turn right. Walk past the mosque until you come to the stall of a handsome young melon merchant"—Zahara sighed—"and ask him to show you Omar ben Allel's house."

Monday, July 31st: "So many proposals! Who would have believed it?" Omar was saying as Musa put down his tea glass for the tenth or eleventh time this afternoon and scratched his head, trying to piece together all of Omar's strange and marvellous news. Omar had summoned Musa to his courtyard for a conference, but so much had happened in Sidi Yussef since Sunday morning that Musa, for once, did not know what to say. First, there was the old woman from the *medina* who had knocked on Omar's door, asked for a drink of water, and promptly

offered him seven hundred and fifty dirhams for
Khadija's hand. Then there was Mohammed ben
Mohammed ben Mohammed's mother, from Sidi
Kacem, who had stopped in Sidi Yussef, on her
way to visit her son at the provincial prison, to
plead with Omar to accept a marriage offer of her
own. No sooner had *she* left, it seemed, than Abdeslam had pulled up in his cousin's truck with a
new caftan for Khadija and a few kilos of mutton
for the family's evening stew. And, finally, toward sunset, the old *medina* lady had come hur-
rying back in a taxi with her son. The son had
turned out to be handsome and young, and—
Allah be praised!—a civil servant. He was, as he
himself had said, an assistant to an assistant to a
construction engineer in the Safi water commis-
sioner's office. His name was Ahmed ben Hassan,
and at the moment he was home in Meknes on
"disciplinary vacation," having punched his im-
mediate superior in the nose in the course of a
heated discussion on the chemical composition of
water. Ahmed had returned to Omar's house
alone this morning, narrowly missing Abdeslam,
who had dropped in with a sack of smuggled
Spanish melons. And then, just before Omar
called Musa to the courtyard and shut his door on
any further complications, Mohammed ben Mohammed ben Mohammed's mother had come back
from the prison to plead her case again before the
bus for Sidi Kacem left Meknes.

With so many visitors, Omar and Dawia had been running around all morning, plumping pillows, shaking hands, and serving tea and bread. The children, playing in the alley, were still waiting for their lunch, and Khadija, shut up in the red room, was grumbling loudly. Her father had put her in the red room early this morning; it was *hshuma* for a girl to be looked at by her suitors.

"I have changed my mind about the driver," Omar said, finally. "I have decided to pass her off as a virgin to the engineer. Perhaps I will win. Perhaps I will lose. But, Allah willing, I am going to try."

"The engineer will find out," Musa said. "How can he not find out?"

Omar thought for a minute. "Perhaps, if I can get them through the wedding night, the engineer will keep her anyway," he said. "After all, he has offered seven hundred and fifty dirhams."

"But what about the trial?" Musa asked him. "They will be married, and then, one day, the judge will knock on your door and say 'Where is Khadija? We are having the trial today.'"

Omar shrugged. "I will go to the Palais and demand a trial this week, before the wedding."

Musa shook his head.

"Then I will go to the Palais and say, 'Forget the trial,'" Omar told him. "I will say, 'I am a kind generous man. I have decided to forgive the

141

prisoner.' " He paused, and added, "Think of the money I will save on Maître Solomon."

Musa shook his head again.

"In that case, when Khadija is called I will say that my daughter is on a trip," Omar began again. "Again then I will go to Safi and tell the engineer that Dawia is sick and needs her daughter for a few days. So he will never know."

"No, no, no," Dawia said, walking into the courtyard with some fresh mint leaves for their tea. "That is not the way to do it at all. What you should say is that you are a working man with ten children and that it is necessary to marry off your daughter right away. You must tell the judge that you are too poor to stay home from work all day guarding her.

"I will say that the rest of my children are starving," Omar agreed.

Dawia sat down. She was talkative today, and as happy as Musa had ever seen her. As she herself told him, there was not another mother in Sidi Yussef who could boast of three offers for a damaged daughter. "The engineer wants the marriage right away, this weekend, at our house," she said.

"Then all the money that he gives you will be gone by Monday," Musa said sourly.

"But I am not looking for money," Dawia said. "I want this man for my daughter. Yesterday, he told me, 'I am not just marrying the girl, I am marrying the faces of her parents, too. It is because I see that you have good faces that I am going to take her.' " Dawia looked proud.

Musa frowned. "What the engineer meant is that you are poor and will be grateful to get a daughter off your hands," he said. "He knows that when he fights with Khadija and she runs home crying, you will not be so anxious to let her in."

"He earns a lot of money," Omar interrupted.

"Well, then, what did he bring you this morning?" Musa asked him.

Dawia blushed, and Omar sighed and said, "Nothing. Not even a sugar cone. We always have the same luck. It is that way with Fatna's husband, too."

Musa cleared his throat and sat up very straight to give his opinion. "Let the driver have her," he said. "Now you are thinking only of the seven hundred and fifty dirhams, but you will see —you will lose more, in the end, with the engineer."

"Perhaps," Dawia said, reaching for Jmaa, who had just crawled over from a corner, and swinging the baby up onto her back.

"It is true that the driver comes with presents," Omar said slowly. "He comes every day. Even today, he gave fifty dirhams to Khadija. He slipped them under the door to the red room."

Dawia agreed that the driver did give many presents.

"You see, he is already a member of the

family," Musa told her. "The other one, this engineer—in the end he will come to you and say, 'I asked for a virgin, not a woman.' What will you say then?"

Omar thought for a moment. "This new one is better," he said. "The driver *knows* that she is not a virgin. He will never give a *sdaq*. He says that it is up to the prisoner to pay."

"And it is difficult to know when and how the prisoner will pay," Dawia added.

"But the *engineer* will pay," Omar went on. "The engineer knows nothing."

"What kind of man is this engineer, that he cannot tell a virgin from a woman?" Musa said.

Omar began to sigh again. "Perhaps you are right," he said. "Saturday we will have the marriage, and by Sunday morning he will know the truth. And even if he does not know, he will hear the gossip."

Dawia shook her head. She would make a magic potion, she said, that was guaranteed to close the ears of the engineer to all the gossip in Sidi Yussef. "If he hears the truth, there will be great *hshuma* for everyone," she told the men.

"Perhaps it is better to give Khadija to the driver after all," Omar said sadly.

Dawia glared at Musa. Then she turned to her husband. "Look at the sky," she said. "If you do not hurry, you will miss your prayers."

Omar put his glass down and began to hunt around the courtyard for his jellaba.

Musa stood up to go. He always stood up to go when Omar left for the mosque, as Omar did faithfully three times a day, except in emergencies. Musa was demonstrating to Omar that he was a man of honor and had no designs on Omar's wife.

Omar, as always, told Musa to sit down. Musa was more than a brother, he said, and Musa, above all men, had his confidence. Then he left the house, smiling. After many years of friendship, neither Omar nor Musa would think of dispensing with their ritual. It was extremely gratifying to both of them.

Dawia watched her husband leave, and then she beckoned to Musa and began to whisper in his ear. "There will be no problems," she said. "I know some magic. You take cloves, and pound them, and mix them with water . . ."

Musa, looking delighted, took in the recipe. His own wife never talked to him about women's magic, although he knew she practiced it wholeheartedly. He himself knew a good deal of men's magic. Once, during his carefree bachelor days in the mountains, he had enslaved the heart of a widow of fourteen through a dark, complicated process involving the bones of a male pigeon. He also knew how to extricate himself from the inconveniences of an impotence curse, should he ever inspire one. And, like Omar, he sprinkled salt on his threshold every night and every morning to keep devils away.

"And so he will never know that she is not a virgin," Dawia concluded.

"But what will you tell the driver?" Musa asked her. "Do you have something for him, too?"

Dawia clucked at him. "Oh, no," she said. "Omar will say that we have heard he has been visiting the father of another girl. That is always a good excuse." She added that Khadija was very happy with the engineer, whom she had seen through the keyhole of the red room and found to be much more beautiful than Abdeslam. Abdeslam, after all, was the color of a sheep's liver.

"There is no denying that," Musa said.

Just then, Omar came back from his prayers. He had run all the way from the mosque, and by the time he reached the house he was panting and breathless. "I cannot do it," he blurted out. "It is better to tell the truth. I saw it all, praying." He flopped onto a pillow and went on, "I will have to tell Ahmed that my daughter is only thirteen and that she is too young to marry. I will say that the judge would never accept such a marriage, no matter how much bakshish was involved."

"That is very sensible," Musa said.

Khadija, behind the door of the red room, started crying.

"But Ahmed is so beautiful," Dawia said.

"Now I will never get to wear a miniskirt or go to Safi," Khadija bawled, pounding on the door. She had not been out of the house since last Monday, when Madame Hugh took her riding through the *ville nouvelle* and bought her chocolate-ice-cream cones. She was getting fatter, but her disposition was worse than ever.

"Perhaps I should tell him that there is another man who wants to marry my daughter, and that they will both have to wait until she is at least fourteen for me to decide between them," Omar said.

"Who is going to have to wait?" The Widow Rabha's voice came hissing through the courtyard door. Omar, in his haste, had forgotten to close it.

No one answered the Widow Rabha. She had been in and out of the house all day, trying to discover what was going on. "I have come for my couscous platter," she announced at last, walking in.

Dawia pointed to the kitchen. She had been using the platter since the day the Widow Rabha cooked couscous for her, when Omar was in Sidi Kacem, but she had hoped that Rabha had forgotten it by now.

The Widow Rabha picked up her platter and started toward the door. Then she stopped, turned on her hennaed heels, and sat herself down between Musa and Omar.

Musa rolled his eyes. He did not approve of women who forgot their modesty. Only last week, he had complained to Monsieur Hugh that the business with Khadija was ruining manners in

147

Sidi Yussef. Women—even the Widow Rabha—
were sitting down with men in their neighbor's
houses. Men were sitting down with women.
There was too much gossip and not enough good
sense.

"Well, what have you decided?" the Widow
Rabha asked.

"We have decided not to do it," Omar said.

Dawia frowned.

"You should do it," the Widow Rabha said.
"It's a good chance. He's handsome. And an engineer."

"You know our problem," Dawia told her.
"You know that the girl is not a virgin."

"And it is more complicated than that," Omar
cut in. "There are problems on all sides."

"I know women who have had five children and
are still given away as virgins," the Widow
Rabha told him. "There are things that can be
done."

Omar poked Musa. Then, smiling at the
Widow Rabha, he said, "Do you want us to pass
him on to you for your Azziza? Why not bring
her over when he comes?"

Khadija banged on her door. "He's mine!" she
shouted. "He's mine!"

"My daughter doesn't want him," the Widow
Rabha said. "We have too many offers to choose
from as it is. The son of her paternal uncle, who
is a rug merchant—"

"What is a rug merchant to an engineer?" Omar said, still smiling. "Why not try? You said yourself that he is very handsome."

The Widow Rabha stood up, clutching her platter. "Perhaps I *will* try," she said.

"Our daughter is young," Dawia told her. "If she doesn't marry this year, then, Allah willing, she can always marry next year."

"But your daughter—your daughter is not so young," Omar said.

The Widow Rabha walked out, and everybody laughed.

"I have changed my mind again," Omar said. "I am going to give Khadija to Ahmed. It would be a shame to waste an engineer on Rabha's daughter." Then he called Khadija out of the red room for a glass of tea.

Tuesday, August 1st: There was a saying in Sidi Yussef that one bad seed was enough to spoil the whole pomegranate. Fathers there, tending as they did to regard their marriageable daughters as pomegranates of sorts—worthless when damaged, but in the right, ripe condition commanding a price far beyond the price of any other fruit—never tired of quoting it. Omar himself had once been exceptionally fond of the saying. Often, sitting by his door on a summer afternoon and watching a neighbor's daughter walk to the market alone, he had shaken his shaved head and murmured, "One bad seed, only one bad seed." Lately, however, he had been reflecting on another saying—one that was equally true and, to his mind, much more consistent with his present situation. This saying went, "From the outside, it is impossible to tell whether the pomegranate is spoiled or not."

"You know what they say," Omar remarked as he and Musa strolled home from the sugar *souk* this morning. "From the outside of the pomegranate, it is impossible to tell anything."

"But you know what they also say," Musa replied.

Omar stared at the ground. The engineer had just come back to Sidi Yussef with his mother to make arrangements for the wedding, and Omar had fled to the *souk,* saying that he was out of sugar for their tea. He wanted time to practice what he was going to tell them.

"It is better to tell the truth now, before there are any problems," Musa said.

"But what can I say?" Omar asked him. "What can I say?"

"What do you want to say?" Musa said. "It is not for me to decide."

"I am going to tell the story just as it happened," Omar said.

Musa nodded.

"But the problem is that I cannot tell it myself," Omar went on. "That would be *hshuma*."

The men walked on, thinking.

Suddenly, Omar stopped. "I have the solution," he said. *"You* are going to tell the story for me."

Musa jumped, as if Aisha herself had crossed his path.

"You are a man of the world," Omar told him.

Musa beamed. "Well, why not?" he said, finally. "For a man of the world, it is not so difficult."

"Tell the son first, then the mother," Omar said. Then he took Musa by the hand and pulled him home.

Ahmed ben Hassan was stretched out on the finest cushion in the *bit dyaf* when the men walked in. He was a lanky young man of twenty-five, with a wide grin and a head of shaggy brown hair that came flopping down across his forehead. He had been training it to flop that way for a year now—ever since the day he saw a newspaper photograph of the famous American Robert Kennedy pinned to the wall of a Safi barbershop.

Musa looked him over. Monsieur Hugh had said that no modern civil servant would send his mother bidding on a bride he had never seen, but Ahmed looked to Musa like a thoroughly modern assistant to an assistant to an engineer. Musa could tell by Ahmed's sweater, which was a fuzzy

gray pullover with cable stitching down the front.
He shook the young man's hand approvingly.

Ahmed's mother, whose name was Yemna,
was squatting across the room by Dawia and the
children. She was all tangled up in a clashing as-
sortment of shawls, scarves, and towels, and,
when Musa stooped to greet her, she giggled and
chattered and clapped her hands. Her eyes were
bright black. Her smile was as wide as her son's
and as toothless as little Jmaa's. The topnotch on
her scarves was the perkiest topnotch that Musa
had ever seen. He told Yemna that she was a
very jolly old woman.

"She is crazy, like a child," Ahmed said cheerfully.

Yemna agreed.

A few minutes later, Ahmed and Musa were
alone. The children had been hustled up onto the
roof to spread the laundry, and the women had
gone into the red room to see Khadija. Omar
himself was in the courtyard. He had told Ahmed
that he was going to pray. Musa, in the *bit dyaf,*
looked around nervously. He was eager to tell
his story right away and get it over with, but
Ahmed had already started talking. Ahmed had
heard about Musa's American patron and wanted
Musa to know that he was looking for a way to
travel to his patron's country. The Americans, it
was rumored, had a wonderful form of hospi-
tality called a United States State Department

Leadership Tour. People said that even the Pasha of Meknes was hoping to go to America on such a tour.

Musa sneezed as Ahmed leaned toward him and he caught the pungent smell of an American hair tonic. "Well, the Pasha is certainly a leader," he said. The Pasha had the confidence of the King, who had been his comrade when they were both boys and the Pasha was summoned to the Lycée Royal as a fitting schoolmate for His Majesty. The King, in fact, had given Meknes to the Pasha as a token of the great friendship between them. Everybody knew, Musa said, that the Pasha could have had the whole province, or even a federal ministry of his own. Meknes, by itself, however, had presented such unique opportunities for exploitation that the Pasha had modestly declined all higher offices. By now, just a few years after his appointment, the Pasha's power and his command of bakshish were the envy of every other pasha in Morocco. He wore three-toned ventilated shoes from Italy and went to embassy parties in Rabat, where he drank wine and ate exotic canapés and walked through gardens with blond secretaries in short skirts. According to Madame Hugh, who had once spoken to the Pasha, he took a great interest in the pleasures of America.

Ahmed told Musa that he was very interested in the pleasures of America, too.

Musa, who had just spotted Omar crouching outside the window of the *bit dyaf* and frantically beckoning, took a deep breath and said, "You know, Khadija—"

"Khadija?" Ahmed said.

"Khadija, whom you are going to marry," Musa said. "Someone stole her from the *musem* of Sidi Ahmed Dghughi. She was gone for three weeks, and then we found her. It was in Sidi Kacem—"

"Where is the man?" Ahmed interrupted.

Musa told him that Mohammed ben Mohammed ben Mohammed was in prison.

"Is there a medical report?" Ahmed asked.

Musa nodded.

"Well, what did they tell her father?" Ahmed went on. "That she is still a virgin, or not?"

"One hundred per cent not a virgin," Musa said.

"Now, then, what are the rest of the problems?" Ahmed demanded.

Musa looked at him, astonished. "Well, nothing," he said. "That is, those are all the problems there are." He paused, and then added, "The girl's parents wanted you to know the truth before the marriage. They did not want to show you one face today and another tomorrow. As you yourself have said, it is not the girl but the face of her parents that you are going to marry."

Ahmed thought for a minute. "I will marry her

anyway, even with all these problems," he said.

Out in the courtyard, Omar jumped up and waved happily through the window of the *bit dyaf*. Musa groaned.

"I hope that you have heard the problems we have had!" Omar called in.

"I have heard them all," Ahmed said, laughing. "There is nothing to worry about."

Omar ran to the red room and called for Yemna. Then, when Yemna also knew the story, he called Khadija and Dawia.

Khadija walked into the *bit dyaf* in a green caftan with a gilded belt. Abdeslam had brought it over early this morning, on his way to Sidi Slimane with a truckload of oranges.

"This is Khadija," Omar said.

Ahmed and Khadija shook hands.

"How do you do?" Ahmed said.

Khadija was blushing, and before she could answer, her father sent her to the kitchen for some fresh tea.

"Well, now you have seen the girl," Omar told Ahmed.

"We accept her, we accept her," Ahmed said. "I know that sometimes things happen to a girl when she is very young."

"Those things are nothing—we accept her," Yemna said, giggling.

"Actually, she is like the pomegranate," Omar said, "We do not really know for sure if—"

Musa groaned again.

"Virgin or not, I will marry her," Ahmed said.

Dawia smiled at him. "Good," she said. "If you really want to take her, you do not have to give the whole *sdaq.*"

"Because she is like the pomegranate, and you are taking a chance on whether she is spoiled," Omar added.

"No, no," Yemna said. "We have promised and we will give it all. We will go for the marriage act tomorrow."

Khadija, walking in with the teapot, threw herself in Yemna's lap and kissed the old woman's hands.

"She will be a good daughter to me," Yemna said, pinching Khadija's cheeks until the girl winced. "Not like the other one."

"The other one?" Omar and Dawia said together.

"Ahmed's other wife," Yemna said. "We have just divorced her."

"Because of my mother," Ahmed added.

Musa looked up from his tea. "Because of my mother" was not a very modern thing to say.

"Because she did not want me to live with them in Safi," Yemna said.

"And because she was not a good mother to my three sons," Ahmed said glumly.

Khadija sat up and, for the first time, took a long look at her future husband.

"Sons?" Omar said.

"But Khadija will be a good mother and look after them," Yemna told him. "And she will help me clean and sew and make the bread and—"

"Since we divorced my wife, there has been no one in the house to help my mother," Ahmed said.

Khadija started to speak, but Omar saw her and said quickly, "Ah, my friends, you have nothing to worry about. My daughter will make all your burdens small."

"That which is heavy for you is light for my daughter," Dawia added.

Khadija frowned.

"We give you the girl, not for the money but to ease your burdens and the burdens of your mother," Omar told Ahmed.

"Be sure that the girl will have a good life with us," Yemna said. "We will do all that is necessary for her."

Ahmed leaned over and slapped his mother on the knee. "You are mad," he said. "Only Allah can do *all* that is necessary. It is Allah who has written the names of the boy and the girl who are to marry."

"Praise be to Allah!" everybody said.

Wednesday, August 2nd: Late last night, Mokhtar and Mustafa waylaid Abdeslam on the road from Sidi Slimane and announced, with great satisfaction, that their older brother was negotiating to give Khadija to an engineer. Abdeslam swore for a while about the gifts and the money he had brought the family. Then he drove his cousin's dump truck to Omar's house, banged on the door, and, as soon as the neighbors were awake and listening, shouted up to Allah that his honor and the honor of his ancestors had been offended. Finally, he left for the *medina,* where he proceeded to celebrate until daybreak with one of his favorite prostitutes.

Ahmed was now the only fiancé Khadija had. He arrived this morning with his mother to sign the act of marriage, and Omar, who was relieved to see him, ran all the way to the *ville nouvelle* to ask that Monsieur Hugh conduct their wedding party to the Notary Palace in style, in his blue Opel. Then Dawia, with Jmaa on her back and Khadija, Abderrahman, Ali, Sidi Mohammed, and Saida trailing behind her, went down the alley looking for the local *moqaddem.* She wanted the *moqaddem,* who was the Pasha's deputy in Sidi Yussef, to sign a birth certificate saying that Khadija was fifteen years old. There was a new law in Morocco which said that a girl must be at least fifteen to marry, and it was making all the *moqaddemin* in the country rich.

Dawia got back first, and she found Yemna, in the *bit dyaf,* sorting out a wad of money into five-, ten-, and fifty-dirham bills. The money was the first payment on Khadija's bride price. Dawia, who had never seen so many dirhams before, touched the bills with trembling fingers. Abderrahman, Ali, Sidi Mohammed, and Saida also touched the money.

Yemna told them that she had been storing the money in a big house in the *medina,* where Ahmed's twin sister lived with her husband, her

children, and another sister, who was just sixteen. She had put it in a pouch in a box in a chest
in a cabinet in her daughter's *bit dyaf*. Then she
had locked the pouch, the box, the chest, and the
cabinet and hidden the keys, in a bunch, inside her
bloomers.

"My mother is very smart," Ahmed said,
laughing. "Everybody wants to steal my money.
First my wife wanted to steal it. And now my
little sister. She wants to run away, because I
have promised her to an ugly old man."

Yemna giggled.

"My husband's little sister has also been promised to an ugly old man," Dawia remarked.

"How horrible," Yemna said.

"It is horrible, but there is nothing to do about
it," Ahmed said philosophically. "These things
are Allah's will."

"That is true," Dawia said. "Daughters are a
problem. When Khadija was stolen, I couldn't
eat or sleep. I was always unhappy."

"I have six daughters," Yemna said. "Six
daughters are enough for anyone."

Just then, Omar, looking disappointed, walked
in with Madame Hugh. Monsieur Hugh had
been busy working, and Omar was not at all convinced of the propriety of being escorted to the
Notary Palace by a woman, especially by a
woman in a short skirt. Yemna, however, was delighted with Madame Hugh's skirt. She in-

spected it carefully, peeking under the hem to
see if the *nesraniyya* was wearing bloomers. Then
she pulled Madame Hugh down onto the floor
and kissed her mouth with a hearty, smacking
sound. Omar said that it was not every family
that had *nesrani* friends with blue Opels.

"When will you have the wedding?" Madame
Hugh asked Ahmed, whom she was looking over
with a good deal of curiosity.

"Well, today we will sign the marriage act, and
then, Allah willing, Saturday we will have the
wedding," Ahmed said.

"That is certainly quick," Madame Hugh said.

"Why procrastinate?" Ahmed said. "Why
drag things out? I have wasted too much money
in restaurants already. I need a wife to cook for
me, and besides, in Safi, my mother and my sons
are alone in the house all day, with no one to wait
on them." He frowned. "Women in Safi do not
like to work for their husbands," he said. "My old
wife—if I told her to make the bread, she would
take my money and go to the bakery instead. If
I told her to sift the couscous, she would say,
'What is wrong with couscous from the *souk?*'"

"It is that way with Safi women," Yemna said.
"They have too much contact with the Europeans."

"But I am used to a wife," Ahmed went on.
"I do not like being a bachelor."

"Being a bachelor is too expensive," Yemna
said.

Ahmed stretched his long legs and checked his wristwatch. In a minute, he was leading the wedding party down the alley to the road where Madame Hugh had parked her car.

Dawia, who had to stay home with the children, watched them from the door, waving with one hand, clutching Ahmed's money with the other, and crying for joy.

The wedding party was halfway to the *medina* when an old man with a lame leg hobbled into the road and hailed the Opel. The man was a friend of Omar's from the coffeehouse in Sidi Yussef, and, as it happened, he had been walking to the coffeehouse now to look for Omar. He said that he had just received working papers from a tire factory in the south of France, but that the Pasha's assistant in charge of passports was refusing to give a passport to him. It was clear, he said, that the assistant in charge of passports merely wanted some bakshish for himself and the Pasha before he would sign a passport order. The problem, however, was that he himself could not present the bakshish. To do so would be bad manners. *Good* manners, in such a situation, demanded that a third man slip the bakshish to the Pasha's assistant. That way, neither the assistant nor the old man would be shamed before each other if they ever met again. Omar, the old man went on, would be doing him a great and never-to-be-forgotten kindness if he would take the bakshish to the Pasha's assistant. Omar, who was feeling exceedingly benevolent today, stepped out of the Opel for a moment to discuss the details with the old man. As soon as his back was turned, Khadija seized Ahmed's hand and stared at it lovingly.

"I have forgotten to ask her," Ahmed said to Madame Hugh. "Does the marriage please her?"

Khadija, blushing, turned away.

"Oh, I would say very much," Madame Hugh said.

"*Very* much?" Ahmed asked her.

Madame Hugh nodded.

"Good," Ahmed said. He glanced at Khadija, who still was clinging to his hand, and added, "I see that she is very friendly."

Omar, who had just come back to the car, said, "Friendly?"

Madame Hugh drove on, shaking her head.

The Notary Palace was, in fact, a little palace, tucked away behind the Bab Mansour and shaded by the *medina's* towering walls. A hundred years ago, its tiled floors, its arched promenades, and its cedar doors and intricately carved ceilings had pleased a sultan's favorite, and caids and concubines once frolicked by the fountains in its flowering courtyard. Today, the notaries, scribes, and judges of the Malikite court kept office hours in the concubines' old bedrooms, off the courtyard, where they presided over all matters concerning marriage, divorce, and family status and prop-

erty, respected an uneasy truce with the judges
of the country's Code Napoléon, across town, and
managed to produce confusions of jurisdiction
and authority that were extremely profitable to
everyone. Women, as they often told their peti-
tioners, were one thing that no good Muslim
would ever trust to the justice of the Europeans.
Women were tricky creatures, barely responsible,
and the divine and clarifying hand of the Prophet
would always be needed for their supervision.

Three old secretaries of the *qadi*—the Malikite
judge—were in charge of the palace when the
wedding party arrived. They were sitting in a
row in the middle of a lovely panelled chamber,
and when Omar and Ahmed approached them
with the ladies, they nodded in unison, giving au-
thoritative little swings to the tassels on the red
fezzes they all wore. Behind them, on the wall,
there were photographs of Mohammed V, the
King's dead father, in a starchy white jellaba,
and of the young King himself in a wrinkled European suit and a graying shirt with a frayed collar. Ahmed shook hands with the secretaries. So
did Omar and Madame Hugh.

"Well, now, who is going to marry?" the secretary in the center said, eying the bare knees of
the *nesraniyya* with a scowl of disapproval. He
was a fat old man with long, gleaming fingernails
and pink jowls.

"I am," Ahmed said. "This is the girl"—he

pointed to Khadija and then to Omar—"and here is her father."

Omar grinned nervously and handed the secretary the birth certificate that the *moqaddem* had written out and stamped this morning.

One by one, the secretaries peered at the piece of paper.

"Very good," the secretary in the center said, rummaging through his jellaba pockets and producing a green plastic ball-point pen.

Khadija looked at him demurely as he asked Ahmed to list the marriage terms.

"Wait a minute! Wait a minute!" the secretary in the center shouted suddenly. He peered at the birth certificate again, and then showed it to his two colleagues. "Is the girl a virgin or is she already married?" he asked Omar.

Omar shuffled his feet on the tiled floor.

The secretary in the center turned to Khadija. "What is the name of your first husband?" he asked her.

"The girl was never married," Ahmed said. "That is certain."

The three secretaries frowned. "This girl is not a virgin, she is a woman," the secretary in the center said, holding out the certificate.

Ahmed took it. In very small letters, next to Khadija's name, the *moqaddem* had written out the word *siyida*— "woman."

The secretary in the center took the certificate

back. A woman was a wife, he told Ahmed. The Prophet had said so. No one could be a woman and not be married. It was not only immoral and even illegal, it was impossible. There was no word for such a woman in Malikite law.

"Perhaps the *moqaddem* has made an error," Omar said hopefully.

"That is no concern of ours," the secretary in the center said.

"The *moqaddem* makes no errors," the secretary on his right added.

Ahmed bent down over the secretaries. "There has been a little problem," he whispered. "What the *moqaddem* meant to say is that there has been this little problem. There is a case at the Tribunal—"

The secretary in the center sniffed. "It is fine for the Tribunal to make these distinctions between women and women," he said. "But we do not acknowledge them. It is very simple. If the girl is a woman, then she has a husband. And if she wants to remarry, she must come back with a divorce certificate, or with twelve witnesses who will swear that she is divorced, or—"

"Yes?" Omar said.

"Or with a new certificate from the *moqaddem*," the secretary said, waving the wedding party from his office. "One that says she is a virgin after all."

Omar, Ahmed, and the women backed out

quietly. Then they all began to talk at once. Omar said that now he would either have to bribe the *moqaddem* to write that his daughter was a virgin or go to the Palais de Justice and bribe the prosecutor to write that she was, in fact, *siyida* but had been divorced.

He preferred bribing the prosecutor, he said, because it would be helpful to have the prosecutor's friendship when Mohammed ben Mohammed ben Mohammed's case came up in court.

Ahmed, on the other hand, wanted Omar to bribe the *moqaddem.* "If you go to the Palais de Justice and say that you want to give away your daughter, the prosecutor will make us wait a hundred days," he said. "That is *his* law. A girl who has been stolen must wait a hundred days to marry."

"To see whether she is pregnant," Madame Hugh explained.

Yemna started giggling. It was *hshuma* for a woman to say such things in the presence of men.

"We will go to the *moqaddem,*" Ahmed said stubbornly. "A hundred days is too long for me to eat in restaurants. I cannot wait a hundred days to get a woman in the house."

Thursday, August 3rd: All day yesterday, the Widow Rabha and her five daughters sat in their courtyard kneading bread and mending caftans while they waited for Omar to cross the alley and formally present them with the handsome engineer. Taking Omar at his word, Rabha had squeezed Azziza's ample body into a silvery caftan. She had circled the aging virgin's chins with all the family beads and necklaces. In a moment of enthusiasm, she had even dusted her cheeks with a chalky, seductive powder made of ground stones.

Today, Azziza was back in her old gray caftan, and the Widow Rabha, cursing her perfidious neighbors in the name of Allah, the Prophet, and Sheikh el Kamel, was plotting her revenge. She was watching through her open door when Omar left this morning for the Palais de Justice— Omar had finally convinced Ahmed that it was wiser to take their problems to the prosecutor— and she was still watching, at noon, when a taxicab pulled into the alley and deposited Fatna in front of Omar's house. Fatna had come home to borrow the family's best blanket, which her husband wanted to take to the beach at Casablanca on his annual vacation from the Sidi Said Hospital. She had also come home, as always, to complain. Her husband, who did not want Fatna to miss a week of valuable practice at stenographers' school, was refusing to take her on vacation with him, and her sister, it appeared, was marrying an engineer who not only was rich and handsome but was willing to pay the girl's entire bride price by himself. Life at the moment was more than usually unkind to Fatna. She was sniffling loudly as she stepped out of the taxi, wearing a pair of bright purple pedal pushers such as the Widow Rabha and her five daughters had never seen.

The Widow and her daughters slid toward their door, grinning.

"Whore!" Azziza screamed, pointing a fat finger at the purple trousers.

"Pig!" Fatna screamed back, running into her parents' house and slamming the door.

A group of Sidi Yussef women stopped on their way to the water pump and waited for the fight. Seconds later, the door opened. Dawia walked slowly into the alley, with Jmaa at her breast and Abderrahman beside her.

"What did your daughter say to my daughter?" Dawia called over to the Widow Rabha.

The Widow Rabha put down the caftan she was mending and stood up. "Your daughters are not like the daughters of good families," she said.

"My daughters are as good as any woman's daughters," Dawia said quietly.

"It is shameful to have daughters who wear pants and who disappear," the Widow Rabha said, nodding with satisfaction to the women who were listening. "Everybody knows about your daughters."

The women stepped closer. Some of the neighbors opened their doors, and the men in the coffeehouse around the corner put down their cards.

"If my daughters disappear, it is not your business!" Dawia shouted. "Pay attention to your own daughters! Keep *them* in the house!"

"My daughters are always in the house, but *you*, you are the mother of whores!" the Widow Rabha screamed.

Abderrahman picked up a stone from the alley

and flung it at the Widow Rabha. The stone
missed Rabha, but it bounced off one of the men
from the coffeehouse, who had just come filing
out to watch the women fight.

Dawia quickly shooed Abderrahman back into
the house. "I know that you are jealous!" she
called to the Widow Rabha. "You are jealous because my daughter was stolen and had many
problems and, even so, has found a husband who
is an engineer, a husband who is handsome and
young. Your daughters have no problems, but
everyone knows that not one of them has found
a husband."

"My daughters are *good* girls," the Widow
Rabha whimpered.

The Widow's five daughters, huddled in their
doorway, nodded modestly.

The neighbors looked at them, but then they
turned to look at Fatna, who had just come out
again. Fatna had covered her face with a thick
black veil, and she was wearing her mother's
jellaba over her purple pants.

"You have been bothering me for a long
time!" Fatna shouted at the Widow Rabha.
"And now you say to my mother that her daughters are not like other daughters! Well, I ask you,
who was the real father of *your* daughters? Who
was he?"

All the neighbors gasped, and the Widow
Rabha, her eyes bulging, ran at Fatna and began

to tear at Fatna's hair. Two men from the coffeehouse pulled her away, just as Omar turned into
the alley and saw the crowd.

Omar was whistling. He had put his problem
to the prosecutor, and the prosecutor had agreed
that Khadija should be married immediately. He
had written all the necessary papers, he had
shaken hands with Omar, and then—to Omar's
great joy and amazement—he had categorically
refused a bribe. Omar had hurried home at once
to tell his wife the news. When he saw the people
in his alley—there were forty or fifty neighbors
watching the fight by now—he waved and smiled,
hoping to be invited to a wedding or a circumcision feast. Then he heard the Widow Rabha
shouting. He pushed through the crowd, grabbed
his wife and daughter, and shoved them back into
the house.

"What are you doing now?" he said, turning to
the Widow Rabha.

"I have nothing to tell you," the widow said.
"Anything that I could tell you, you already
know. *Everybody* knows."

Omar looked around at all his neighbors.
"Why do you listen?" he shouted. "If what she
says is true, you are all experts on what has happened to my family!" Then he looked at the
Widow Rabha. "Ask them," he said. "Perhaps
they can tell you something. Perhaps you will discover more gossip for your wicked tongue."

The Widow Rabha glared at Omar. "I know that my meals do not give pleasure to my neighbors," she told him. She was still talking about the platter of couscous she had made for Dawia.

"Aha!" Omar shouted. "So you regret the couscous! Well, tomorrow I will make *three* platters of couscous and leave them at your door!"

All the people in the alley laughed and clapped.

The Widow Rabha stamped into her house, furious, but in a minute she was back. "Tell me, what kind of a neighbor are you?" she screamed at Omar. "I do not want such a neighbor!" Then she threw back her head and shouted to the hot noon sky, "I demand that Allah separate us immediately!"

Omar waved his hand at the Widow Rabha. "We are separated!" he shrieked. "You have your house and I have mine! But you—you are not content to live only in your house! You live in your house *and* in mine! It is because of *that* that there are always problems!"

"Allah will punish you!" the Widow Rabha shrieked back. "We have shared our tea, and now you have broken the friendship! You will be punished!"

Omar shrugged. "You ask Allah to separate us," he said. "And then you ask Allah to punish me." He started laughing wildly. "But now we will wait and see who is going to be punished. We will see which family is the first to leave this quarter."

"I am ashamed to talk to you!" the Widow Rabha shouted. "My family has never done the terrible things your family has done!"

Omar approached her, screaming. "Each person belongs in his *own* house!"

The Widow Rabha fled to her doorway. Omar turned on his heel and walked slowly across the alley to his house. He bolted the door, but he could still hear the Widow Rabha shouting.

"Our doors are not far enough apart to end relations," Dawia, who was waiting in the courtyard with the children, told him.

Omar shook his head sadly. "It is just as I have always said," he murmured. "It is a burden, having daughters. Even now, it is a terrible burden."

Friday, August 4th: Khadija and Ahmed began their wedding today. The fight with the Widow Rabha had persuaded Omar to give his daughter to the engineer as quickly as possible. He had been hoping to put off the celebration for a few days, to give Ahmed more of an opportunity to buy presents for the family, but he knew that now the widow would be busy spreading her gossip, and he feared that in time her stories would reach Ahmed and make him change his mind. Early this morning, he rushed Khadija to the *medina*

179

in a taxi and proudly presented Ahmed with
her divorce from Mohammed ben Mohammed
ben Mohammed, stamped by the prosecutor and
dated exactly one hundred days ago.

At 9:01, in the Notary Palace, under the pious
gaze of the *qadi* and the *qadi's* three secretaries,
Omar solemnly pressed his thumbprint onto his
daughter's act of marriage.

It was an odd contract, as the *qadi* remarked,
although it was not nearly so odd as the marriage
act that he had witnessed a year ago for Fatna
and Driss. Ahmed agreed to pay in full a *sdaq* of
seven hundred and fifty dirhams, but, inasmuch
as Ahmed argued that it would be unreasonable
for Omar to expect two bride prices for the same
daughter, Omar himself agreed to pay back to
the engineer whatever money, up to but not ex-
ceeding the seven hundred and fifty dirhams, and
less the fees of the powerful Maître Solomon, the
Tribunal saw fit to extract from Mohammed ben
Mohammed ben Mohammed's relatives.

Omar was not entirely content with the agree-
ment. What with bribes, taxi fares, bills from the
shurwaf, and sugar and tea for half the old
women in Sidi Yussef, Khadija's problems had
already put him in debt for more than three hundred dirhams, and now, on top of everything, he
had a wedding feast to give. Ahmed's *sdaq* would
cover these expenses, but Omar, who was anxious
to buy his mule, had been counting on some extra

money from the prisoner. In fact, he was of the opinion that a fat, healthy mule was just the sort of compensation he deserved for all his sufferings. Still, no mule was worth another day with Khadija shut in the red room and complaining about swimming pools and abandoned caftans. Omar was finally getting rid of another grumpy, troublesome daughter, and he put his thumbprint to the act of marriage with a smile on his lips and a kind word for Allah in his heart.

Once the marriage act was sealed, the wedding party had a busy day. Ahmed ran around the *caesaria*—the street of fabric stalls in the *medina* —trying to locate tailors who would make Khadija's bridal robes by sunset, when his mother and his sisters were to carry them on their heads to Sidi Yussef, stopping along the way for the neighbors to appraise and admire his generosity. Khadija herself was paraded to the *hammam* by three old women to be bathed, hennaed, and shaved for the festivities. Dawia baked bread and started to prepare a sugary wedding couscous. Abderrahman, Ali, Sidi Mohammed, and Saida went scampering down the alley with invitations for all the neighbors but the Widow Rabha and her five daughters. And Omar walked to the goat *souk* to bargain down the price of a young male goat for the nuptial sacrifice. The wedding goat was actually the responsibility of the bridegroom, but Ahmed had said this morning that he refused to buy one. "No virgin, no goat," he had told Omar. And Omar was obliged to agree that there was much justice in what his new son-in-law had said.

By early evening, Omar was standing at his door, waiting to receive the women of Ahmed's family and their gifts. He knew that they were coming soon. Ahmed himself had come an hour ago to see the goat, and had proceeded to stuff it into the trunk of a waiting taxicab and send it to the *medina,* where it would lead the procession of women back to Sidi Yussef. It would bring great *hshuma* to them both, he had explained to Omar, if the neighbors along the ladies' route were able to say that Ahmed ben Hassan was too unfeeling to provide his own wedding goat. Ahmed, at the moment, was sitting comfortably in the *bit dyaf,* chatting with Monsieur Hugh about the trials and the advantages of married life.

Omar could just make out, somewhere in the distance, the music of the flutists and the drummers who were accompanying the goat, the women, and the wedding caftans on their slow, proud journey through town, and he yelled into the house for Dawia and Madame Hugh. The women came out of the kitchen, where they had been kneading extra loaves of bread for the feast tomorrow, to wait with Omar at the door. Madame Hugh was covered from head to foot with flour. She had been kneading dough since early

morning, when Dawia, who was afraid that the
Widow Rabha would persuade one of the neighbors to poison everybody at the wedding, had announced that, of all the women in the city, only
the *nesraniyya* would be welcome in her little
kitchen to help with the preparation of the bridal
dinner. Such poisonings were not uncommon, as
Dawia had explained to the American. She had
heard of one this very week in Sidi Yussef. It had
been prompted by jealousy, like the jealousy of
the Widow Rabha, and had sent an entire circum-
cision-breakfast party to the Sidi Said Hospital.
Now, at the door, Dawia gestured knowingly
across the alley; the door to the Widow Rabha's
house was firmly and pointedly closed. Then she
waved at Musa, who had also heard the music and
was trotting down the alley to join his friends.

"It is time to buy the honey and butter for the
musicians," Dawia was saying when Musa arrived.

"So it is poor Omar, after all, who is going to
pay for everything," Omar said, looking gloomy.
"It was Omar who bought the goat, and look—
now they are leading it here as if it were *their*
goat."

"People do those things," Musa remarked. "I
know a man who borrowed twenty-five sacks of
sugar and fifteen sacks of farina at the *souks* before his wedding. He had them driven to the wedding in a big cart, for everyone to see, and then,

that night, he returned them all while his guests were busy with the wedding feast."

"But I am spending all my money," Omar complained. "All my money from France. All of my daughter's *sdaq*—"

Dawia frowned at him. "Ahmed is spending money, too," she said. "Today, he spent four hundred dirhams just for caftans and jewelry."

"Yes, but it is Ahmed, not Omar, who is getting married," Omar said.

"Omar, you attack me," Dawia said, laughing. Then she turned to Madame Hugh. "Nothing can begin without the honey and the butter," she told her. "That is the custom."

"As the butter and the honey are sweet, so shall the life of the two lovers be sweet forever," Musa added, with appropriate solemnity.

Madame Hugh reached into her big brown pocketbook and pulled out ten dirhams with her floury fingers. Musa took the money and left to buy the honey and the butter.

Omar looked relieved. "Wait until Zahara's wedding," he whispered to Madame Hugh as Musa disappeared up the alley in the direction of the butter merchant. "You will never get honey and butter at my brothers' house."

"Mokhtar and Mustafa are very selfish," Dawia said.

"You will see," Omar went on. "The poor musicians won't even get a glass of tea for their troubles. And the neighbors will get nothing to eat."

"It is *hshuma*," Dawia said. "So many presents from Bushta, and they won't even spare a glass of tea."

"*Hshuma*," Madame Hugh agreed, smiling.

"You will never see a wedding as fine and happy as the wedding I am giving for my daughter," Omar said. "Even if she is not a virgin."

Dawia put a finger to her lips and nodded down the alley. Mokhtar and Mustafa were coming toward them. Mustafa, dressed in his fine gray suit and tattersall vest, was on the family mule, and Mokhtar was walking beside it in his baggy trousers and his torn undershirt.

"Abderrahman has come to us with an invitation," Mustafa said as soon as the brothers reached the doorway.

Dawia smiled. "I invite you to the marriage of my daughter," she said.

The brothers were speechless. Mustafa stared at Omar with his mouth open, and Mokhtar toed the ground, kicking at stones.

"This husband you have found—you have told him all the problems?" Mokhtar said. "You have explained everything?"

Dawia nodded.

"He is young and handsome and an engineer," Omar said. He glanced at his brothers and added, "And rich. Much richer than the one you have chosen for our sister."

Mustafa squirmed on his mule. "You really have explained everything?" he asked Omar.

"*I* am a man of honor," Omar said. "And he is a modern man. He understands these things that happen. He does not approve of locking virgins in the house all day, without exercise. He says that it is bad for their . . . for their . . ."

"For their circulation," Madame Hugh suggested.

"Exactly. Bad for their circulation," Omar said.

Mustafa looked down at Omar and Dawia. "Very well, then, we will assist you at the girl's wedding," he said grimly. Then he punched the old mule's rump. The mule bucked and took off down the alley, with its long ears flopping in the evening breeze. Mokhtar ran after it, shouting to Mustafa that it was his turn to ride.

Omar and Dawia watched them go, laughing and pointing and nudging Madame Hugh. Jmaa, who had just crawled out of the courtyard, cooed, oblivious, until the *nesraniyya* picked her up. There was a large open sore on one side of Jmaa's mouth which looked to Madame Hugh like the beginning of yaws. Driss had painted it with gentian violet last night, on his way out of town for his vacation. He had charged only a dirham, as he was hoping to appease Omar, who had just learned that Fatna would not be coming to the wedding, and who was threatening to take his blanket back. Fatna had sent a message to her father. Khadija, the message went, was more than a *hisha mwusskha*. Khadija not only had disgraced the family, she had been the cause of Fatna's great humiliation in the alley yesterday afternoon. Fatna would rather stay home with her mother-in-law in the *medina* and practice her stenography than dance at the wedding of such a terrible girl.

Dawia, seeing Madame Hugh with the child, blushed into her towel and said in a low, confidential voice, "Ahmed is a just man. He did not ask that we bring Khadija to him tonight, even though it is his privilege, now that the marriage act is signed. He said that he would wait until the proper wedding."

"He is anxious enough to begin his amusements," Omar said.

Dawia clucked at him. "And Ahmed is good and thoughtful," she went on. "He says that we will have the marriage exactly as if the girl had not been stolen. He says that he knows the neighbors will be waiting."

"You are crazy," Omar said, glaring at the Widow Rabha's closed door. "The neighbors know everything."

Dawia ignored him. "Just this morning, Ahmed said, 'I am going to make your faces proud and happy at the wedding,'" she told Madame Hugh. "He said, 'You will have no shame in front of the neighbors.'"

Omar shrugged. "How?" he said.

"Ahmed said that tomorrow night he will come with a pigeon and a sharp knife," Dawia whispered, lowering her eyes. "Do you know what he is going to do? He is going to slaughter the pigeon, and then, when the wedding is over, all the neighbors will see that there is blood on my daughter's bloomers."

"Bloomers?" Omar cut in. "What is this nonsense about bloomers. You cannot show bloomers to the neighbors. It is not proper. It is the *sheet* that you must show."

Madame Hugh suppressed a grin.

"Ahmed says that sheets are for peasants to show," Dawia told him. "He says that civilized people, in the city, show bloomers."

"Bloomers—it is not right," Omar said.

"You are not a shepherd anymore," Dawia said. "You are getting an engineer for a son-in-law. It must be bloomers."

"Sheets," Omar said.

"Bloomers," Dawia insisted.

Then they turned to Madame Hugh. Madame Hugh said that she wanted to consult her husband on the question of bloomers. She handed Jmaa to Dawia, and then she ran into the *bit dyaf,* where Ahmed and Monsieur Hugh were drinking tea and smoking cigarettes by candlelight. Ahmed was telling Monsieur Hugh about his younger sister, who had brought many problems to the family. This sister, whose name was

Naima, had been permitted to marry a young man of roughly her own choosing. The young man had divorced her when she turned sixteen and was beginning to show signs of wear. "It was her own fault," Ahmed was saying. "What can a woman know about selecting husbands?" In the end, he had had no choice but to promise her to an old man. "Ah, the poor, poor girl," Ahmed said, with feeling. "She despises him."

"But who arranged this awful marriage?" Madame Hugh asked him, walking in and sitting down on the floor.

"Why, I did," Ahmed said, looking surprised. "There was nothing else to do with the poor girl. Certainly she could not stay in the house unmarried—"

"Not even until you could find a nice young husband for her?" Madame Hugh interrupted.

Ahmed shook his head. "There would be trouble—she has been married once and she can no longer be trusted," he said. He turned for support to Monsieur Hugh. "Everyone knows that once a girl has been married, even for a single night, she can never be trusted to guard herself again. Some man will meet her at the *souk* and offer her a present, and she will follow him." Then he sighed. "So, you see, it was necessary to find a husband for my sister while there was still time," he said. "But I am lucky. I have found a man who wants her. Next week, we will have the marriage."

"I think that's very cruel," Madame Hugh said.

"But you do not understand," Ahmed said. "Moroccans are different from the *nesraniyyin.* You *nesraniyyin,* you do not have to lock up your wives. But here, if I do not lock up my wife, a man will open my door and she will go with him. And bring me great *hshuma.*"

"Poor Khadija," Madame Hugh said. "She will never get to go swimming after all."

Monsieur Hugh poked her.

"I have heard that in your country even a man who sees a woman dancing does not follow her," Ahmed said. "That would never happen in Morocco." He looked at Monsieur Hugh and added, "I have seen it all at the movies. The men in America think of nothing but business. But here no one thinks of business. We think only of stealing women. We are very virile, very hot-blooded."

Monsieur Hugh shrugged.

"And the women here are not like the *nesrani* women," Ahmed went on. "The women here will shame their husbands for a few dirhams. They love money."

"All women love money," Monsieur Hugh said.

Ahmed thought for a moment. "Ever since my

divorce, I have been spending money on women,"
he said. "There was one—I walked with her one
day, and then I asked her parents to make the
marriage. They agreed, but they demanded a
sdaq that was unthinkable." Ahmed paused. "After all, I had already walked with her," he said.
"Twice."

Madame Hugh stood up, brushed some of the
flour off her blue jeans, and left the room without
a word about Khadija's bloomers.

Ahmed watched her go, shaking his head.

"It is difficult to explain, but in America men
and women have the same rights," Monsieur
Hugh said, smiling. "They are considered . . .
equal."

Ahmed slapped his knee and laughed. "Oh,
that is very good," he said.

"Well, what happened to the girl?" Monsieur
Hugh asked him.

"I said no to her parents, of course," Ahmed
said. "I told them that I would never marry their
daughter, even if she came free."

Monsieur Hugh chuckled.

"That is why I sent my mother here, to the
bidonville," Ahmed went on. "I said to my
mother, 'Show me a poor girl and I will show you
a scandal in the family.' "

Monsieur Hugh looked confused.

"You see, I wanted a girl who was young and
had been in trouble," Ahmed explained. "I knew

that then there would be no problems with money. No stories. No disobedience. I knew that a poor girl would always obey me, because I had rescued her. And I knew that her parents would be grateful. I knew that if I beat her she could not run home, because her parents would bolt the door and tell her, 'Go back to your husband, who has rescued you.' "

Ahmed sat back, contented, as the sound of flutes and drums and singing filled the alley. Then, when the procession reached the house, he leaned over and shut the door. It would not be modest, he said, to show himself to the neighbors with so many of his gifts around.

Outside, Omar and Dawia welcomed the women of Ahmed's family. Yemna came first, leading the goat by a rope and balancing the bundle of wedding caftans on her head. There were five caftans in all. Khadija would wear them, layer on layer, throughout her wedding, in stuffy tribute to her husband's generosity.

Yemna tilted her head, and the bundle tumbled to the ground at Dawia's feet.

Dawia examined the caftans, exclaiming loudly so that the neighbors, standing at their doors, could hear her. "Ah, five beautiful caftans!" she shouted.

Omar nodded energetically. "Five beautiful caftans!" he yelled.

"And two beautiful pairs of shoes," Ahmed's

twin sister, Hada, said, dumping her bundle at the feet of the happy parents.

"Two beautiful gold belts, three nightgowns, and a European pin!" Naima called out, adding her own bundle to the pile.

Dawia scooped up the clothes and ran into the red room, where Khadija was sitting with a jagged piece of mirror, smearing some of Madame Hugh's blue eye cream across her eyelids. Madame Hugh, behind her, was combing the snarls out of Khadija's long black hair. She took the bundles, and Dawia ran back to the alley to greet the musicians.

There were four musicians in the wedding procession. Two of them were drummers. The other two carried elegant little flutes made of apricot wood. For the moment, they had all stopped playing and were pacing back and forth before the doorway, waiting for their butter and honey. In honor of the occasion, they had skipped lunch.

Dawia beamed at them. "You see, Ahmed has paid for *two* flutes," she said to Omar.

Omar nodded glumly. Now *he* was obliged to pay for two flutists for the feast tomorrow. There would never be an end to his expenses, he whispered to Dawia. Then, as Musa turned in to the alley holding up a big package, he invited the musicians into the house for honey and butter. The neighbors shut their doors, satisfied.

Abderrahman dragged the goat up the narrow

stairs that led from the courtyard to the roof, where it would soon be sacrificed and skinned and hung to dry. Dawia took the women into the red room to help put Khadija into her five new wedding gowns.

Ahmed, in the *bit dyaf,* closed his eyes. "Well," he said. "It has finally started."

"Praise be to Allah," Monsieur Hugh said.

Saturday, August 5th: All the wedding guests arrived this afternoon. Musa was the first to come. Fresh from a nap, he walked proudly up the alley, his black turtleneck sweater still damp from a scrubbing in a bucketful of Tide, and his black hair smooth and shiny with a touch of olive oil. Habiba followed him to the wedding at a respectable, wifely distance, with a daughter cradled in each of her plump arms and a prospective son bulging under the dark jellaba that was shielding her bright, red Berber party clothes from the scrutiny of Arab alley boys. Mokhtar and Mustafa came next, with *their* wives and children, and their father and mother. Zahara, unaccustomed as she was by now to going walking, stumbled along behind them in a pair of stiff new shoes. Then Bushta came, armed with a stick and uninvited, to defend his fiancée against the melon merchant, who stayed home. The neighbors came in huge families, trailing babies and grandmothers and distant cousins. Yemna came, on foot, with Ahmed's Meknasi sisters and his three small sons. And Ahmed's friends from the *medina* came by taxicab, alone, muttering to one another about the huts in Sidi Yussef and the unpaved roads.

Finally, just as the sun dropped out of sight behind the sacred mountain where Khadija had been stolen, Monsieur and Madame Hugh turned in to the alley in their car. Monsieur Hugh had added a necktie and a plaid jacket to the blue shirt and khaki pants he always wore to Sidi Yussef, and Madame Hugh had abandoned her blue jeans and little skirts for a long, silky orange dress that turned miraculously into trousers when she moved around. Madame Hugh told Dawia, who was very much impressed with this exotic costume, that it was called a culotte and was worn by ladies across the ocean in the city of New York.

Some Moroccans would say that it was bad

luck for men to look at the women at a wedding. Others would say that it was *haram*—forbidden —in the eyes of Allah. But most Moroccans would say that women at weddings were simply too beautiful to be safely seen. All the young women and the virgins at Khadija's wedding came oiled and hennaed and drenched to a steamy allure with their favorite perfume, which was called Nuits Arabes. Silvery bracelets jingled on their arms. Plastic beads from the *medina* glittered at their throats. It was clear to them all that, in their perfume and jewelry and shimmering acetate caftans from the *caesaria,* the young women of Sidi Yussef were much too beautiful to be looked on, and only when they were closeted in the red room with Khadija did they throw off their veils and their gray jellabas and step into the candlelight to admire each other.

Madame Hugh, in her culotte, walked into the courtyard, where Yemna and the old women of thirty-five and seventy sat, like vigilantes, with the small children, burning incense and gossiping about the price of chickens and the price of brides. Then the door to the red room opened, and a bare brown arm reached out and pulled the *nesraniyya* inside. Monsieur Hugh, at the edge of the courtyard, watched her disappear into the makeshift harem. He stood there for a while, smiling bashfully at the old women, but when the

197

old women youyoued disapprovingly he ran up the stairs to the roof to join the men.

Omar's roof was chilly after the closeness downstairs, where the smells of sweat, acetate dyes, moist henna, Nuits Arabes, and babies had mingled with the burning incense to produce a pungent, nearly suffocating incense of their own. Only this morning, the *shuwwaf* had remarked to Dawia that the forty days of heat, which had come to Meknes at the time Khadija was stolen, would end tonight, in honor of the girl's deliverance. Omar had laughed at the prediction—"If he is blind, tell me, how can he count?" Omar had asked when his wife came home—but now he was forced to admit that the *shuwwaf,* for once, had told the truth. A sharp westerly wind was blowing over the city, and the men on Omar's roof, who had come to the wedding in their thinnest summer jellabas, were huddled together on little rugs and blankets, trying to keep warm.

"It is just as the *shuwwaf* said!" Omar called to Monsieur Hugh when the American's head popped up out of the dark stairwell. "The *smaym* has gone. It is a good omen."

Monsieur Hugh shivered, and he took his place on one of the striped Berber blankets Musa had donated to the wedding decorations. Around him, the men, in their small huddles, were talking together softly, ill at ease. The wedding of a *siyida* was an awkward occasion—even the old men of

Sidi Yussef, who sat in a corner warming their
hands at a brazier, seemed at a loss for the proper
protocol. They stared into the brazier or out over
the neighbors' rooftops and did their best to ignore the mutterings of Ahmed's friends. Only
Musa kept his eyes on the young men from the
medina. They had stationed themselves on one of
Musa's finest blankets, and not one of them had
remembered to take off his shoes. Musa was ready
to snatch his blanket out from under them. He
was waiting for the first smudge.

Ahmed, sitting with his friends, was also trying
to ignore their comments. First they had snick-
ered at Omar, in his post-office uniform, and now
they were passing the time until dinner joking
about the poverty of the quarter and about the
cheap tea they were drinking and the raggedy
condition of everybody else's clothes. Ahmed, for
the third time tonight, was explaining to them his
reasons for choosing a wife in Sidi Yussef. His
first wife had been lazy, he said. Money meant
nothing to her. She never worked to get the best
prices at the vegetable *souk,* and once she even
spent a dirham at the tailor, having his pants
mended, rather than mend them herself. Ahmed's
friends nodded, looking glum.

Mokhtar and Mustafa, meanwhile, were
spending a quiet evening in a dark corner of the
roof. Mustafa, who on arrival had crumbled a
little chunk of hashish into his mint tea and al-

most immediately passed out, was lying on his back, snoring peacefully. Mokhtar, who had shared the tea, was squatting on his heels, grinning at everyone. Their father, next to them, pretended that Mokhtar and Mustafa were not around. Allel had come to the wedding with his mangy prayer rug, and at the moment he was waiting for the muezzin at the mosque to climb to the roof with his bullhorn and wail out the invocation to evening prayer. He had just asked his aging future son-in-law to check the time again.

Bushta, standing in the corner, put down his stick and consulted a gleaming, chromium-plated pocket watch. He could not tell Allel when the prayers would start, but he knew from the giggles and shrieks of the little boys who were hanging over the big square opening in the middle of the roof that it was time for the virgins and the young women to come out of the red room and begin their dancing. He seized his stick, waiting for one of Ahmed's friends to make a move. When none of the young men budged, he brandished his stick regardless and hollered into the night that he himself was going to guard the opening.

The little boys scattered, laughing. Three of them were Ahmed's sons. They had lost their old mother, in accordance with the Prophet's law, when Ahmed divorced her, but they had just had a look at a new mother with bright-blue eyelids

and five beautiful wedding gowns. Earlier, they
had also had a look at Abdeslam, the driver, who
was lying in the alley getting drunk on a forbidden bottle of Meknes burgundy. Abdeslam
was still celebrating.

Down in the courtyard, the young women and
the virgins settled into a wide circle on the floor
and took the tall clay drums that Dawia was
handing out of the red room. Khadija got the
first drum. It was an enormous purple *gwal,* and
it rocked and slid around when she tried to rest it
on her shoulder. Finally, Khadija kicked off her
new white shoes, squatted barefoot on the floor
tiles, and clamped the *gwal* firmly in place between her knees. She rolled up the drooping
sleeves of her outermost caftan—a white, satiny
caftan stamped with pink and yellow rosebuds.
She rubbed her smarting eyelids. And she began
to play.

Dawia, beaming, shooed the children into the
bit dyaf for a nap on the mattresses that she had
stitched together for the consummation of Khadija's marriage.

One by one, the young women and the virgins
stood to belly dance. Habiba danced first, because
Naima, who had never seen a Berber belly dance,
pulled her, protesting, into the center of the
circle. But Habiba could barely move a muscle
of her swollen belly, and soon Naima started
dancing herself. She was a plump, rosy girl with

201

a tangle of black ringlets on her forehead, and she danced on and on around the circle while the rest of the women youyoued with pleasure and banged their drums. Then, coming to Zahara, she held out her hands. Zahara shook her head, reached up under Naima's swishing caftan, and tried to pull her bloomers down. Both girls tumbled to the floor, laughing.

"My new husband is going to be older and fatter and uglier than yours," Naima shrieked, tickling Zahara in the ribs.

Zahara howled, rolling her round brown eyes in the direction of the roof. *"Mine* is worse," she said. "Go up and see for yourself."

Naima, still laughing, crawled over to Madame Hugh. "It is Allah's will—what can I do?" she asked the American lady. Then she grabbed Madame Hugh by the hand and dragged her into the center of the circle. She wanted to learn a beautiful American dance, she said. Ahmed had seen it in the movies, and Madame Hugh, perhaps, had seen it too. It was called "the Twisting."

To claps and youyous and the beat of the big clay drums, Madame Hugh began to dance. The old women, sitting along the courtyard walls, stared in terror at the thumping, jerking spectacle, and even Dawia, who had gone back to the kitchen to guard her couscous from treachery, came out to watch. In a minute, all the virgins and the young women but Khadija were busy learning Twisting from Madame Hugh. For a bride, dancing was very *hshuma.*

Suddenly, the old women along the walls began to youyou excitedly. Out in the alley, the wedding musicians had just signalled their arrival with a wail of flutes, and the men were running down the stairs to welcome them. The young women and the virgins turned away demurely when the men ran by. The old women covered their faces with their shawls.

Omar was the first man out the door. He had paid two drummers and two flutists for the evening, and now, in his honor, the drummers and the flutists were serenading Omar with the wedding music from his native village. They stood at the door playing as the men filed out. Then, grinning, they stepped aside, and a large, perspiring young woman with kohl-rimmed eyes and a mouth that was nibbled to a brilliant crimson came dancing out of the darkness up to Omar. The young woman was a *shikha,* a dancing whore who travelled from city to city, *souk* to *souk,* and pilgrimage to pilgrimage with a troupe of wandering musicians. Her mother, who was retired from travelling, ran a small brothel in Meknes, and the *shikha,* whenever she was homesick, liked to pass through town and pay a visit to her mother's house. Omar was one of her oldest clients. Today, she had heard the news about his daughter's wedding and, out of respect for the family, she had decided to come out to Sidi Yussef to entertain his guests. As soon as all the men in the alley were singing and dancing to the wedding music, she offered her arm to Omar, and they began to dance. Then she danced with Mokhtar, who was also one of her admirers. So, in fact, was Mustafa, but Mustafa, as Omar had noted with satisfaction, was still snoring in his corner of the roof. Omar watched Mokhtar and the *shikha* dancing for a minute, and then, with a host's prerogative, he snatched the lady from his brother and danced her around the alley again.

An hour later, Dawia opened the door a modest crack to say that the wedding feast was being served.

Madame Hugh was still Twisting when the *shikha* walked into the courtyard, hand in hand with Dawia. It was clear that she startled the *shikha* with her strange dancing and her orange costume, because the *shikha,* dropping Dawia's hand, pulled Madame Hugh down onto a pillow to examine her. The *shikha* admired the miraculous trousers, as well as the pearly-pink paint on Madame Hugh's toenails. Then, showing the *nesraniyya* her tattoos, which covered her forehead, her chin, her arms, her legs, and her ankles, she announced to the women that she was going to perform her special wedding dance. All the women and the virgins clapped.

The *shikha* stood up, smoothed the skirt of her

gauzy caftan, and marched around the courtyard.
Finally, by the kitchen door, she spotted one of
the bottles of Sidi Ali's holy water, which Khadija was going to drink tonight to insure a fruit-
ful marriage with many male children. She held
up the bottle for the women to approve. Then,
placing it under her caftan, she danced over to
Khadija and began to sing.

The young women and the virgins rolled
around on the floor, laughing. Soon they were all
singing with the *shikha*. Yemna and the old women were singing. Dawia, back in the kitchen,
was singing. Even Khadija, who had been sulk-
ing about her lost opportunity to learn Twisting,
was singing as the *shikha* jiggled the bottle of
holy water up and down. None of the women
heard Abdeslam pounding on the door and hollering that he had come to claim the bride—Abdeslam, after his second bottle of burgundy, had
stopped celebrating and started regretting—and
none of them noticed Omar and Ahmed race
down the stairs to drive him away. Abdeslam left
the alley with a black eye just as the *shikha* com-
pleted the last stanza of her wedding song.

Up on the roof, the men sat shivering around
clay platters and dug their fingers into the wedding couscous and the goat stew. Ahmed's
friends, alone on Musa's blanket, were grumbling
about the meal, which they said was not up to
medina standards as a wedding feast, but Bushta,

who had already eaten his way through two platters of stew, was belching contentedly. Omar,
prowling around the roof with a flashlight to see
to his company, announced to no one in particular
that this was the finest wedding he had ever been
to. He scooped up a handful of couscous from
the platter that the Sidi Yussef men were shar-
ing, smacked his lips loudly, and then walked
over to the corner to wake up Mustafa. The
women, downstairs, had started eating, and soon
it would be time for Mokhtar and Mustafa, as
the bride's paternal uncles, to stand in the middle
of the courtyard and call on the wedding guests
for gifts.

With Mokhtar's help, Omar managed to get
Mustafa on his feet and down into the courtyard
by the time the women finished eating. Dawia had
just come out of the kitchen with a bowl of wet
pounded henna, and Zahara, kneeling before
Khadija, had rolled up her sleeves and was ready
to apply it to her niece's hands and feet. All the
women were youyouing. They crowded around
Khadija, making a screen of shawls and caftans.
Then Zahara solemnly dipped her hands into the
henna and reached out for the bride's right foot.

"Who has the first present for Omar's daughter?" Mokhtar shouted.

One of the Sidi Yussef women tossed him a flat
silvery box. There was a pretty picture of Mary,
the mother of the *nesrani* prophet, on the cover of

the box, but Mary's face had been replaced by a piece of cellophane to reveal—"Praise be to Allah, what have we here?" Mokhtar shouted—a long yellow nylon nightgown in two layers.

Everybody murmured approvingly. The Virgin Mary's nightgowns were highly prized in Sidi Yussef. They came all the way from Spain to the *medina,* where they could be purchased at five dirhams a layer, and they were considered wedding presents in impeccable taste. Five more women passed their boxes of nightgowns over to Mokhtar. He opened them all, and held up each of the nightgowns for the other women to admire.

"Thank you in the name of Allah!" Mokhtar called over the din of the youyouing.

"And in the name of the Prophet," Mustafa added, staggering around the courtyard. "And in the name of Sidi Ali, Sidi Ahmed, Sheikh el Kamel, Moulay Idriss—" Mustafa tripped over one of the old women and fell down. In a minute, he was snoring again. Omar and Dawia dragged him into the kitchen to sleep.

"And who else is going to give?" Mokhtar said, leaping into the middle of the courtyard and calling up to the men on the roof. Several hands reached out over the opening, clutching coins and bills. A shower of dirhams bounced off Mokhtar.

"Five dirhams from Hassan ben Gdar!" a voice from the roof called down.

"Ten dirhams from the family of Labid ben Yussef," another voice said.

"Five dirhams from Hassan ben Gdar, ten dirhams from the family of Labid ben Yussef!" Mokhtar shouted. "May Allah bless you! May all the saints of the land bless you! May Sidi Ali and Sidi Ahmed and Moulay Idriss bless you!"

Zahara dipped into her bowl and reached for Khadija's left foot.

The *shikha* marched up to Mokhtar, with a toss of her damp black hair, and slapped five dirhams into his outstretched palm. Mokhtar made an appointment for Tuesday afternoon.

Suddenly, a fifty-dirham bill floated down into the courtyard.

"Fifty dirhams from Bushta," came the deep, cracking voice of Zahara's fiancé.

Mokhtar jumped up and down in his torn undershirt, waving the money for all the wedding guests to see. "Fifty dirhams from the fine Bushta, the generous Bushta, the worthy, honorable, beautiful Bushta!" he shouted.

Omar looked stunned. He turned to Dawia, at the kitchen door, and whispered, "Bushta must be very happy to have his driver back."

"Everything is for the best," Dawia said.

The hennaing went on. By the time Zahara set aside an empty bowl and wiped her hands on her caftan, it was two in the morning, and Mokhtar had collected more than a hundred dirhams and eleven nightgowns. The women had settled down in the courtyard to wait grimly for the consummation of the marriage, and the men, up on the roof, had settled down to wait for tea.

Dawia scooped up the money on the floor, tied it in a rag, and stuffed it into the bosom of her caftan, where it swung around slowly, like a bulky pendulum. Then, dragging a dozen sleepy children from the *bit dyaf,* she dusted the mattresses for Khadija and Ahmed. At first, when Ahmed had announced that he was actually coming to his own wedding, instead of waiting with his friends in the *medina* for his bride to be delivered to him, Dawia had said that such a wedding was a bit *hshuma.* Even Yemna, who knew that her son was saving money that would otherwise go to feed a second dinner to the wedding party, had acknowledged that it was not done. But now Dawia looked proud that Ahmed was going to spend his wedding night in Sidi Yussef. Humming to herself, she lit a tall white candle that was standing on the floor in a broken saucer. Then she called softly to Khadija, who left the courtyard, modestly sobbing.

Khadija took her place on the bridal mattresses. Dawia covered her daughter's face with a long shawl and laid an odd white package at her side. When she was back in the courtyard, pouring tea and chattering gaily to the women, Ahmed tiptoed down the stairs and into the *bit dyaf* and shut the door.

Half an hour later, Dawia looked up from her glass of tea and let loose a piercing youyou into the early-morning air. The old women, the young women, and the virgins jumped to their feet. Wide-eyed and exclaiming, they raced after Dawia into the *bit dyaf*. Then they began to you-you, too. Even Madame Hugh, who had never mastered the women's art, was youyouing. Ah-med had gone. Khadija, lying on the mattresses in her five wedding gowns, was smiling slyly, and Yemna was standing beside her, balancing a big brass tea tray on her head. Spread across the tea tray, for everyone to acknowledge, there was a pair of very beautiful and very bloody bloomers.

Up on the roof, the drummers and the flutists began to play.

"It cannot be," the old men of Sidi Yussef whispered to one another.

"This is not what we have heard," Ahmed's comrades grumbled.

"This is impossible," Bushta said.

Ahmed and Omar, however, stood before them all, grinning proudly, and Yemna was al-ready up the stairs with the brass tea tray and the bloomers on her head.

Joining the men in a circle around the old woman and the tea tray, Musa proposed the first song of the morning in honor of the bride's virginity. It was a Berber song, from Musa's mountain village, and he sang it once alone, in the high, clear voice of mountain men. "Honor to the bride," the song went. "Honor to the bride like the pigeon that guards its grain under the clove tree."

"There is a saying," Omar whispered to Monsieur Hugh, who had walked up to the circle with his mouth open. "It is that he who speaks last speaks truth."

In a minute, everyone was singing.

FOR THE BEST IN PAPERBACKS, LOOK FOR THE

In every corner of the world, on every subject under the sun, Penguin represents quality and variety—the very best in publishing today.

For complete information about books available from Penguin—including Pelicans, Puffins, Peregrines, and Penguin Classics—and how to order them, write to us at the appropriate address below. Please note that for copyright reasons the selection of books varies from country to country.

In the United Kingdom: For a complete list of books available from Penguin in the U.K., please write to *Dept E.P., Penguin Books Ltd, Harmondsworth, Middlesex, UB7 0DA.*

In the United States: For a complete list of books available from Penguin in the U.S., please write to *Dept BA, Penguin*, Box 120, Bergenfield, New Jersey 07621-0120.

In Canada: For a complete list of books available from Penguin in Canada, please write to *Penguin Books Ltd, 2801 John Street, Markham, Ontario L3R 1B4.*

In Australia: For a complete list of books available from Penguin in Australia, please write to the *Marketing Department, Penguin Books Ltd, P.O. Box 257, Ringwood, Victoria 3134.*

In New Zealand: For a complete list of books available from Penguin in New Zealand, please write to the *Marketing Department, Penguin Books (NZ) Ltd, Private Bag, Takapuna, Auckland 9.*

In India: For a complete list of books available from Penguin, please write to *Penguin Overseas Ltd, 706 Eros Apartments, 56 Nehru Place, New Delhi, 110019.*

In Holland: For a complete list of books available from Penguin in Holland, please write to *Penguin Books Nederland B.V., Postbus 195, NL-1380AD Weesp, Netherlands.*

In Germany: For a complete list of books available from Penguin, please write to *Penguin Books Ltd, Friedrichstrasse 10-12, D-6000 Frankfurt Main I, Federal Republic of Germany.*

In Spain: For a complete list of books available from Penguin in Spain, please write to *Longman, Penguin España, Calle San Nicolas 15, E-28013 Madrid, Spain.*

In Japan: For a complete list of books available from Penguin in Japan, please write to *Longman Penguin Japan Co Ltd, Yamaguchi Building, 2-12-9 Kanda Jimbocho, Chiyoda-Ku, Tokyo 101, Japan.*